Microsoft System Center 2012 Endpoint Protection Cookbook

Over 30 simple but incredibly effective recipes for installing and managing System Center 2012 Endpoint Protection

Andrew Plue

[PACKT] enterprise 🞋

PUBLISHING   professional expertise distilled

BIRMINGHAM - MUMBAI

Microsoft System Center 2012 Endpoint Protection Cookbook

First published: October 2012

Production Reference: 1270912

Published by Packt Publishing Ltd.
Livery Place
35 Livery Street
Birmingham B3 2PB, UK.

ISBN 978-1-84968-390-6

www.packtpub.com

Cover Image by Artie Ng (artherng@yahoo.com.au)

Credits

Author

Andrew Plue

Reviewers

Nicolai Henriksen

Matthew Hudson

Stephan Wibier

Acquisition Editor

Stephanie Moss

Lead Technical Editor

Azharuddin Sheikh

Technical Editor

Kaustubh S. Mayekar

Project Coordinator

Vishal Bodwani

Proofreader

Mario Cecere

Indexer

Monica Ajmera Mehta

Production Coordinator

Arvindkumar Gupta

Cover Work

Arvindkumar Gupta

About the Author

Andrew Plue is a Senior Consultant in the Secure Infrastructure Management group at Certified Security Solutions (CSS). He is veteran of the United States Army, and served as a paratrooper with the 1/508th Airborne Combat Team.

He has 18 years of experience in information security, with a focus on vulnerability detection, and corporate anti-virus solutions. During his tenure at CSS, he has acted as a lead engineer on numerous deployments of the Forefront Suite of anti-malware products, with production deployments of Forefront Client Security as large as 140,000 seats.

He has spoken at the Microsoft Worldwide Partner Conference on the topic of Forefront Client Security.

In his spare time, he does not do all that much, to be honest.

I would like to thank Norah, for inspiring to do more with my life. James and Linda, my parents, for not giving up on me (I was a bad kid). Nicholas, Natalie, Emily, and Jamenson for giving me hope for the future and Maximus, Purrrsy, Melonball, and Machka for keeping my feet warm and my house rodent free.

About the Reviewers

Nicolai Henriksen is working as a Chief Infrastructure Consultant, and has been in the consulting business since 1995 implementing mostly Microsoft systems, but also a wide range of other vendors and products. He has always had a great interest and skills within managing and securing systems, servers, and clients. He has wide experience with most of the malware protection products in the market today. He is also a Microsoft Speaker and has performed several presentations with great demos at Microsoft events and international conferences. He got awarded as an MVP Microsoft System Center Configuration Manager in 2012.

Matthew Hudson has been involved in technology since the early days with the TRS-80 Model III. He has over 20 years of experience in the systems management area, consulting, and programming. Matthew received the Microsoft MVP award in 2009 for his expertise, community involvement, and drive to push the SMS 2003 product beyond the norm. This is his fourth year as an MVP in System Center Configuration Manager. He holds an undergraduate degree in Engineering from Texas A & M University and a Masters degree in Computer Science from Prairie View A & M University.

Stephan Wibier is a consultant and all-around IT geek specializing in Microsoft Backend Services. He has specialized in OS Deployment using tools, such as WDS/MDT and SCCM 2007/2012.

His interest in the IT business goes way back to the early 80s, starting with the good-old Commodore 64. After that, it was only a matter of time before the virus hit hard. He is certified in several areas of Microsoft products and still keeps up with the new and fabulous changes in the modern IT market.

He is known for his pragmatic style, approaching problems as changes or opportunities.

www.PacktPub.com

Support files, eBooks, discount offers and more

You might want to visit www.PacktPub.com for support files and downloads related to your book.

Did you know that Packt offers eBook versions of every book published, with PDF and ePub files available? You can upgrade to the eBook version at www.PacktPub.com and as a print book customer, you are entitled to a discount on the eBook copy. Get in touch with us at service@ packtpub.com for more details.

At www.PacktPub.com, you can also read a collection of free technical articles, sign up for a range of free newsletters and receive exclusive discounts and offers on Packt books and eBooks.

http://PacktLib.PacktPub.com

Do you need instant solutions to your IT questions? PacktLib is Packt's online digital book library. Here, you can access, read and search across Packt's entire library of books.

Why Subscribe?

- ▶ Fully searchable across every book published by Packt
- ▶ Copy and paste, print and bookmark content
- ▶ On demand and accessible via web browser

Free Access for Packt account holders

If you have an account with Packt at www.PacktPub.com, you can use this to access PacktLib today and view nine entirely free books. Simply use your login credentials for immediate access.

Instant Updates on New Packt Books

Get notified! Find out when new books are published by following @PacktEnterprise on Twitter, or the *Packt Enterprise* Facebook page.

Table of Contents

Preface

System Center 2012 Endpoint Protection (SCEP) is Microsoft's third-generation corporate anti-malware solution. At the core, it shares many similarities with their "free for home use" anti-malware product, Microsoft Security Essentials, which has been installed on over 50 million PCs the world over.

The explosion in popularity of the Microsoft Security Essentials benefits SCEP users through the malware telemetry data of 50 million users of the Microsoft Security Essentials that share with Microsoft through their MAPS (formerly known as Spynet) program. By integrating SCEP with the newly-released System Center 2012 Configuration Manager, they have created one of the easiest solutions to deploy and manage anti-malware products on the market.

In this book, you will see System Center 2012 Configuration Manager referred to as simply SCCM. Although Microsoft often refers to it as ConfigMgr in their documentation, the majority of the people the author has worked with over the years refer to the product as SCCM. System Center 2012 Endpoint Protection will be referred to as SCEP, although this is not an official acronym that Microsoft uses for the product.

Many of the recipes in this book begin with a step that asks you to log into your Central Administration Server (CAS). Depending on how your SCCM environment was designed, you may not have a CAS server, you may simply have a single Primary Site server as the top level of administration in your architecture. If this is the case, all the recipes can be completed on your Primary Site server.

Also, in most cases, it is not essential to physically log into the CAS or Primary site server. If you have the SCCM consoles installed on your workstation and are logged in with the correct permissions, the recipe can be performed on the local console.

What this book covers

Chapter 1, Getting Started with Client-Side Endpoint Protection Tasks, provides a number of recipes for performing tasks at the local client level, such as forcing a definition update or modifying the SCEP client policy.

Chapter 2, Planning and Rolling Installation, will walk you through some of the considerations you will need to make before deploying SCEP, as well as showing you how to enable the SCEP role on your SCCM server.

Chapter 3, SCEP Configuration, will show you recipes for performing essential tasks, such as configuring SCEP policies and alerts, as well as walking you through the process of setting up SCEP's reporting features.

Chapter 4, Client Deployment Preparation and Deployment, includes a number of recipes to assist you with every step of client deployment from preparation to actually deploying the clients.

Chapter 5, Common Tasks, covers a number of day-to-day tasks that every SCEP administrator will need to know how to do it correctly in order to keep SCEP healthy and your Endpoints protected from malware.

Chapter 6, Management Tasks, covers important high level tasks, such as using policy templates, merging polices, and responding to SCEP alerts.

Chapter 7, Reporting, makes a deep dive into the reporting capabilities offered with SCEP. You will be shown how to execute reports, as well as provide access to reports. You will also be shown how to create your own custom reports.

Chapter 8, Troubleshooting, provides you with some tools to assist you with the time-consuming effort of troubleshooting an anti-malware product. The recipes in this chapter will help you deal with Definition Update issues, as well as how to approach false positives.

Chapter 9, Building an SCCM 2012 Lab, is a great chapter for anyone who has not yet taken the plunge on SCCM 2012. There is just a single recipe in the chapter that will show you the quickest down-and-dirty method for standing up an SCCM 2012 server in a lab environment. This is vital to anyone considering deploying SCEP, because with the total integration of SCEP with SCCM 2012, you can't experience SCEP without an SCCM environment.

Appendix, walks you through the installation of the System Center Security Monitoring Pack for Endpoint Protection.

What you need for this book

To complete the recipes in this book, you will need a Windows 2008 level (or above) Active Directory environment, a Windows 2008 R2 server, SCCM 2012, and SQL server 2008.

Who this book is for

This book is intended for any SCCM 2012 administrator, who needs to quickly ramp up his or her skill sets in order to support SCEP. It is also intended for anti-malware administrators of an existing anti-malware solution (such as McAfee or Symantec) that needs to learn quickly the SCCM-related skills that he or she would need to have in to manage an anti-malware solution integrated with SCCM.

Conventions

In this book, you will find a number of styles of text that distinguish between different kinds of information. Here are some examples of these styles, and an explanation of their meaning.

Code words in text are shown as follows: "The local SCEP client logs are stored in the `program data` folder".

Any command-line input or output is written as follows:

```
Threat Name:VirTool:JS/Obfuscator
ID:2147632206
Severity:5
Number of Resources:2
Resource Schema:file
Resource
Path:C:\Users\username\AppData\Local\Microsoft\Windows\Temporary Internet
Files\Low\Content.IE5\OG2NNMHR\badwebpage.htm
```

New terms and **important words** are shown in bold. Words that you see on the screen, in menus or dialog boxes for example, appear in the text like this: "Click on **File** from the menu bar and select **Exit** to close the logfile ".

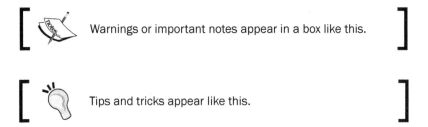

Warnings or important notes appear in a box like this.

Tips and tricks appear like this.

Reader feedback

Feedback from our readers is always welcome. Let us know what you think about this book—what you liked or may have disliked. Reader feedback is important for us to develop titles that you really get the most out of.

To send us general feedback, simply send an e-mail to `feedback@packtpub.com`, and mention the book title via the subject of your message.

If there is a topic that you have expertise in and you are interested in either writing or contributing to a book, see our author guide on `www.packtpub.com/authors`.

Customer support

Now that you are the proud owner of a Packt book, we have a number of things to help you to get the most from your purchase.

Errata

Although we have taken every care to ensure the accuracy of our content, mistakes do happen. If you find a mistake in one of our books—maybe a mistake in the text or the code—we would be grateful if you would report this to us. By doing so, you can save other readers from frustration and help us improve subsequent versions of this book. If you find any errata, please report them by visiting `http://www.packtpub.com/support`, selecting your book, clicking on the **errata submission form** link, and entering the details of your errata. Once your errata are verified, your submission will be accepted and the errata will be uploaded on our website, or added to any list of existing errata, under the Errata section of that title. Any existing errata can be viewed by selecting your title from `http://www.packtpub.com/support`.

Piracy

Piracy of copyright material on the Internet is an ongoing problem across all media. At Packt, we take the protection of our copyright and licenses very seriously. If you come across any illegal copies of our works, in any form, on the Internet, please provide us with the location address or website name immediately so that we can pursue a remedy.

Please contact us at `copyright@packtpub.com` with a link to the suspected pirated material.

We appreciate your help in protecting our authors, and our ability to bring you valuable content.

Questions

You can contact us at `questions@packtpub.com` if you are having a problem with any aspect of the book, and we will do our best to address it.

1

Getting Started with Client-Side Endpoint Protection Tasks

In this chapter, we will cover:

- ▸ Locating and interrupting client-side SCEP logs
- ▸ Performing manual definition updates and checking definition version
- ▸ Manually editing local SCEP policy using the user interface
- ▸ Utilizing `MpCmdRun.exe`

Introduction

The tasks you will accomplish in this chapter are essential for any **System Center Endpoint Protection** (**SCEP**) administrator. Although many of the procedures can also be performed from within your **System Center 2012 Configuration Manager** (**SCCM**) console, it is also vital to understand how to perform these procedures at a local client level. As isolating infected PCs (or PCs that are suspected to be infected) from the rest of your corporate network is a commonly accepted best practice, a hands-on approach is often needed to remediate malware issues.

This chapter will cover all the essential skills an AV admin using SCEP will need to know, from finding and understating the SCEP client logs, to performing on demand scans with just the command line.

Locating and interrupting client-side SCEP logs

Primarily, reporting data is accessed through the SCEP dashboard within your SCCM console, or by executing SCEP reports in SQL Server Reporting Services. However, you may find yourself attempting to troubleshoot a malware issue on a client PC without an access to either of those resources. This is when you come to know where to find your SCEP client-side logs, and understand how to interrupt them, which will prove very useful.

In this section, you'll be working with the most vital SCEP log, which is known as the **MPLog** and using it quickly will locate pertinent information, such as definition update history and malware detection history.

Getting ready

The local SCEP client logs are stored in the `program data` folder. Keep in mind, this directory is hidden by default and you will not be able to browse to it without enabling **view hidden files, folders**, and **drives** in Windows Explorer. A log parsing utility, such as **Microsoft's Trace32** or the new version that comes with SCCM 2012 CMTrace, can be utilized to expedite the process of locating data inside the MPLog, but in the following example, we will be utilizing Notepad.

How to do it...

Follow these steps:

1. To locate your SCEP client-side logs on a Windows 7, Vista, or Windows Server 2008 system, navigate to the following path: `%systemdrive%\ProgramData\Microsoft\Microsoft Antimalware\Support`

2. Open `MPLog-XXXXXXXX-XXXXXX.log` with Notepad.

3. Once Notepad is open, hit *CTRL-F* to open the **Find** window.

4. Type in `Threat Name` to locate a record of malware detection, and press the *F3* key to move to the next instance.

5. Back in the **Find** window, enter `signature updated via` to locate a record of the client's definitions updating.

6. Next, search for `Scan Source` to locate a record of a scheduled scan running or record a running scan that is on demand.

7. Then, enter `Expensive file` to locate an instance of an expensive file detection during a scan.

8. Click on **File** from the menu bar and select **Exit** to close the logfile.

How it works...

While the MPLog contains an abundance of data, the keywords we searched for will allow you to quickly locate some of the most pertinent data.

SCEP supports multiple definition update methods, which will be discussed later. Although the SCEP reports will show you which definition version a client is running, it does not reflect where a client receives its update. You should be able to find entries similar to this: **Signature updated via InternalDefinitionUpdateServer on Sun Jan 02 2011 21:33:50**.

In this case, **InternalDefinitionUpdateServer** would indicate that the definition update was pulled from a WSUS/SUP server within your corporate network.

In addition to this, there are several other entries you may find, such as **Signature updated via MicrosoftUpdateServer on Sat Mar 12 2011 17:54:56**. This would indicate that a definition was pulled from Microsoft Updates over the Internet. This should be common for remote users. Signature updated via UNC \\Servername\share indicates that an update was pulled from a UNC file share.

The MPLog also records any malware incidents the client has detected. If the client has experienced a virus detection, you will find an entry similar to Threat Name:VirTool:JS/Obfuscator. The following lines can provide some more background information about the virus detection, for example:

```
Threat Name:VirTool:JS/Obfuscator
ID:2147632206
Severity:5
Number of Resources:2
Resource Schema:file
Resource
Path:C:\Users\username\AppData\Local\Microsoft\Windows\Temporary Internet
Files\Low\Content.IE5\OG2NNMHR\badwebpage.htm
```

The resource path can provide some very useful information when determining the attack vector or source of an outbreak. In the previous example, the malware was detected in the user's temporary internet files, indicating the attempted infection likely occurred when the user browsed to a website containing malicious code.

To find out what actions the client took after detecting the malware, continue to scroll downwards a few lines, where you'll locate an entry similar to the following:

```
Beginning threat actions
Start time:⊠Fri ⊠May ⊠13 ⊠2011 15:41:51
Threat Name:Virus:DOS/EICAR_Test_File
Threat ID:2147519003
```

```
Action:remove
```

```
File to act on SHA1:3395856CE81F2B7382DEE72602F798B642F14140
```

```
File cleaned/removed successfully
```

```
File Name:C:\Users\username\AppData\Local\Microsoft\Windows\Temporary
Internet Files\Low\Content.IE5\X2GCUOEX\eicar[1].com
```

```
Resource action complete:Removal
```

In this case, the infected file was successfully removed.

The MPLog also records detections of what are known as **Expensive Files**. These are files which take the SCEP client an abnormally long amount of time to scan. Knowing what files are considered expensive can be valuable when tuning your SCEP policies for optimized scanning performance. If your SCEP client has detected expensive files during a scan, you may find a log entry similar to the following:

```
!WARNING
```

```
Expensive file
```

```
File Name:C:\Program Files (x86)\Program\largefile.exe
```

```
File Size:107374882
```

```
Time:6552
```

If you know whether this is a safe and valid file, you may consider adding a custom exclusion for this file in your SCEP policy.

There's more...

In addition to the uses outlined in the recipe, there are other logs generated by the SCEP client that may prove useful to you.

More details about the MPLog

The MPLog is the primary client side log for SCEP. It will contain information on almost every aspect of a SCEP client. The MPLog will have a filename that matches to the following criteria: `MPLog-01012011-174035.log`. In this example, the value 01012011-174035 corresponds to the date and time the logfile was first created, January 1, 2011 at 5:40 pm. Typically the MPLog is created during the installation of the SCEP client.

Other useful client-side logs

The MPLog is not the only logfile which SCEP writes events to; `MPDetection-XXXXXXXX-XXXXXX.log` records an event every time malware is detected.

NisLog.txt

If you've enabled the **Network Inspection System** (**NIS**) component of SCEP in your SCEP policy, then it will append data to `NisLog.txt`.

NIS is the network monitoring component of SCEP. It creates a logfile in the following directory:
`C:\ProgramData\Microsoft\Microsoft Antimalware\Network Inspection`
`System\Support`

 If you've chosen to utilize NIS monitoring, the NISLog on your clients is important, because events generated by the NIS service are not sent to the SCEP infrastructure and therefore, cannot be viewed in SCEP reports.

The NIS service starts during bootup, and creates log entries similar to the following sample:

```
01/03/11-11:23:10] ********************************************
[01/03/11-11:23:10] Network Inspection System service starting.
[01/03/11-11:23:10] Built on "Nov 11 2010" "14:31:02"
[01/03/11-11:23:10] Version: 3.0.8107.0
[01/03/11-11:23:10] ********************************************
[01/03/11-11:23:10] Updating configuration
[01/03/11-11:23:10] [Load  ] Consumer: {fc9058d8-dc9f-4416-bad1-
09a6ad347c2a} IpsConsumer.dll (Type: 1)
[01/03/11-11:23:10] Loading engine from folder c:\ProgramData\Microsoft\
Microsoft Antimalware\Definition Updates\{1BF8C8F4-9AA1-42A8-87CA-
F1A9D94E1034}, fAllowEngineReload=0
[01/03/11-11:23:12] --Signature list start--
[01/03/11-11:23:12] [Off] Sig {887ab750-5912-11dd-ae16-0800200c9a66}
Plcy:Win/SMTP.DNSLookups.RCE!2004-0840 - Signature not Host-Detect or
Host-Block
```

What you can see from this entry is that the NIS service started successfully and loaded its signatures. If the system running SCEP is fully patched, it will not be uncommon to see the most, if not all, of the modules are set to [Off].

NIS is designed to monitor for known network-based exploits and to cease monitoring for a given exploit, once the corresponding **Hotfix** is installed. In other words, NIS is aware of the patch level of the OS it is running on and will not waste resources scanning for attacks, despite the OS being no longer vulnerable.

Performing manual definition updates and checking definition version

All anti-malware clients depend on a constant stream of updates to be successful in protecting against new threats. Depending on how your SCEP policies are configured, it is possible for a user to perform a manual definition update. This section will detail the procedures for updating the client through the SCEP user interface.

Getting ready

Open the SCEP client **User Interface** (**UI**) by navigating to the **Start** menu under **All Programs**, or double-clicking on the SCEP shield icon in the system tray, as shown in the following screenshot:

How to do it...

1. Within the SCEP UI, select the **Update** tab, as shown in the following screenshot:

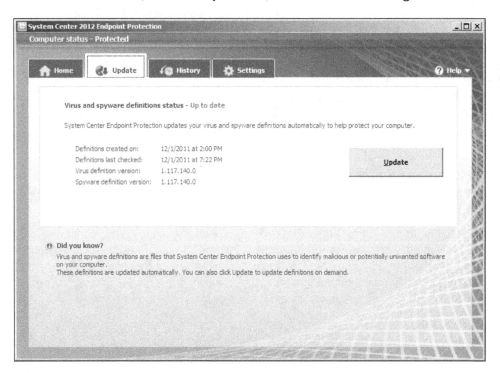

2. Click on the **Update** button to launch a manual definition update.

3. Once the update is complete, the value for **Definitions last checked** should change.

How it works...

If you've built your SCEP policies with multiple update sources, the SCEP client will first attempt to pull a definition update from the source listed first in the policy. If that source is not available, it will default to the second update source in the policy, and so on.

One thing to be aware of is that if your SCEP policy points the clients to an internal resource, such as **Windows Server Update Services** (**WSUS**) that has long intervals for synchronizing with Microsoft Updates, it is possible that your clients won't receive the most up-to-date definition file. For this reason, it's a best practice to set the synchronization interval to a minimum of three times per day.

If you are using WSUS or Microsoft Updates to provide SCEP definitions, an event will be logged in the Windows Update logfile, `%SystemDrive%\Windows\WindowsUpdate.log`. If you are utilizing UNC file shares to provide definitions, the Windows Update logfile will not be updated as the UNC delivery method does not utilize the automatic updates agent component of Windows.

You may have noticed in the previous example that both the virus definition and spyware definition file have the same version number; this is because Microsoft utilizes a unified definition file. Virus definitions, spyware definitions, and engine updates all come in the same package.

There's more...

With something as vital to the security of PC as steady stream of new defintions is fortunate that Microsoft has provided a number of alternate sources. This helps to ensure that if one source of definitions becomes unavailable, then the client can fail over to another source.

Alternate definition sources

In addition to providing SCEP definitions through Microsoft Updates, Microsoft also provides SCEP definitions as a self-contained executable file on their Malware Protection Center website, which is as follows: `http://www.microsoft.com/security/portal/`

The screenshot of the previous link is as follows:

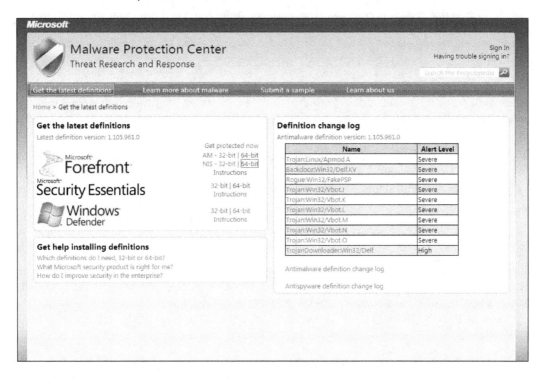

From this web page, you can download either the 32-bit or 64-bit version of the definition file, as well as updates for the NIS service. The file `mpam-fe.exe` (for 32 bit) or `mpam-fex64.exe` (for 64 bit) contains a full update for both the anti-virus and anti-spyware definitions, as well as the most up-to-date engine version. Once the file is downloaded, simply executing it will update your SCEP client automatically.

Microsoft Update opt-in

As SCEP is not considered by Microsoft to be a core piece of OS software, it will be necessary to opt-in to receive SCEP updates through Windows Updates if your SCEP client is attempting to connect directly to Microsoft Updates on the Internet. This is accomplished by opening the **Windows Update** interface in **Control Panel** and clicking on **Get updates for other Microsoft products** and agreeing to the end user license agreement.

This is something to be particularly aware of when creating new images that include the SCEP client. Whether a system has been opted-in or not, it will still be able to receive definitions from internal resources, such as WSUS or UNC file share.

Manually editing local SCEP policy using the user interface

This recipe will detail how to modify the settings of a SCEP client using the **Settings** tab of the SCEP client UI. Although, typically in a large-scale environment, the settings for a SCEP client will be defined in a SCEP policy on the SCCM server, it is useful to understand how to modify these settings at a local client level for testing and troubleshooting purposes.

Getting ready

If a SCEP client is receiving a policy from an SCCM server, or through GPO, the extent to which the local SCEP policy settings can be modified in the client user interface is defined in that policy. A stand-alone SCEP client's setting can be fully modified, although in both cases, local administrator rights will be needed to save changes.

How to do it...

1. To begin, open the SCEP client UI and select the **Settings** tab, as shown in the following screenshot:

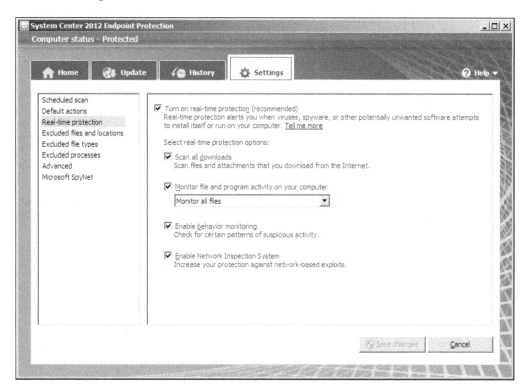

2. Select the **Scheduled scan** menu option to modify the frequency and type of scans.

3. Select the **Default actions** menu option to modify SCEP's reactions to malware detections of the listed severities.

4. Select the **Real-time protection** menu option to modify the behavior of SCEP's real time anti-malware engine.

5. Select the **Excluded files and locations** menu option to add or remove custom file and directory exclusions, as shown in the following screenshot:

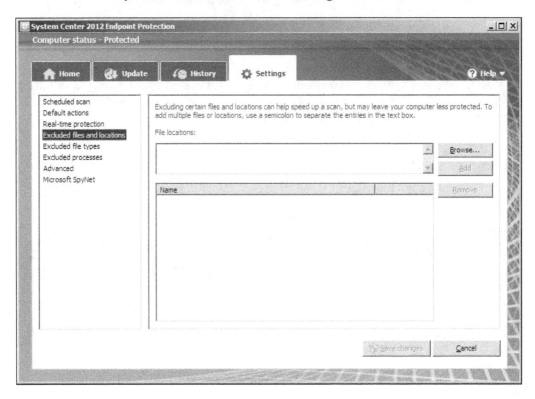

6. Select the **Excluded file types** menu option to add or remove custom exclusions for specfic file types.

7. Select **Excluded processes** to add or remove custom exlusions for specific applications and programs as depicted in the following screenshot:

8. Select the **Advanced** menu option to modify how SCEP handles removable drives, how long it stores files in quarantine, and how long it keeps events in the **History** tab. Refer to the following screenshot:

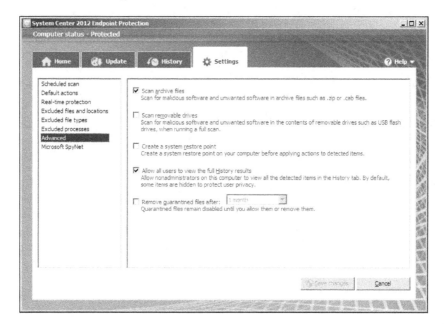

9. Select the **Microsoft SpyNet** tab also known as the **Microsoft Active Protection Service** (**MAPS**) menu option to enable or disable particpation in **Microsofts Spynet** system.

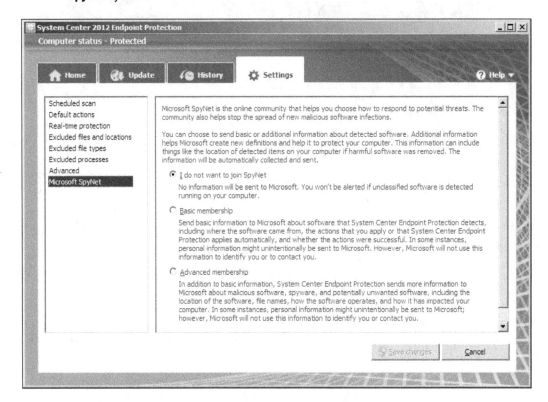

10. Click on **Save changes** to complete your modifications.

How it works...

On the **Scheduled scan** page, you can define the interval for how often a scan will occur and whether it will perform a full or quick scan. You can also disable scheduled scan altogether by unchecking **Run a scheduled scan on my computer**.

Microsoft has also added a couple of options for scheduled scans, which are designed to minimize the performance impact for end users. The **Start scheduled scan only when my computer is on but not in use** option will delay the starting of scan until the system is idle. The **Limit CPU usage during a scan to** setting allows for CPU throttling between 10 percent and 100 percent; this is an especially valuable setting when configuring a SCEP policy for an application or file server.

The next page of settings covers **Default Actions**, which are preset reactions the SCEP client will take when malware is detected. What category a piece of malware will fall into is defined within the SCEP definitions.

If any SCEP policy has been assigned to a PC from SCCM, you will not be able to modify the Default Actions settings locally. A standalone client on the other hand does allow for the modification of the Default Actions settings, which are as follows:

- The **Real Time Protection** page allows you to modify how the anti-malware engine interacts with the OS. Real time protection can be completely disabled here, although it's never recommended to do so, unless you're troubleshooting an issue with a client.

- The **Monitor file and program activity on your computer** setting allows for some performance tweaking on file servers. You could choose to only scan incoming files or only outgoing files. It's recommended to leave this setting at the default setting of **Monitor all files** unless you have an explicit reason to do otherwise, such as troubleshooting I/O performance on a file server.

- The **Enable behaviour monitoring** setting allows you to toggle the **Behavior Monitoring** feature of SCEP. This is a new technology that Microsoft has developed which monitors running processes for suspicious actions that could indicate an infection. For example, a process that loads and then attempts to modify certain sections of the registry known to be favored by viruses could trigger a Behavior Monitoring event.

- **Enable Network Inspection System** allows you to turn the NIS service on or off. As I mentioned earlier, NIS monitors network traffic for patterns that correspond to known vulnerabilities in Windows. NIS is only supported on Windows Vista SP1, Windows 7, and Windows 2008 server systems.

- The **Excluded Files and Locations** page allows for either specific files or entire directories to be excluded from scanning.

When a SCEP client is installed, some preset exclusions will already be defined. Adding additonal exclusions should be done with caution. If a new exclusion is needed, the specific files should be excluded before choosing to exclude an entire directory. The use of wildcards, such as an asterisk (*) and system variables, are allowed.

The **Excluded File Types** page allows you to exclude specfic file extensions. To exclude a file type, simply enter the three-character file extension, such as MDB. A period symbol (.) is not needed and will be stripped out if used. Common file types will have a description added automatically. As a best practice, it is recommended to use file type exclusions sparingly. Adding exclusions for a specific file is more secure approach.

There's more...

The SCEP client has the ability to exclude `.Exe`, `.Com`, and `.Scr` processes. To add an exclusion for a process, you must know the complete path to `.Exe`, `.Com`, or `.Scr`. The path can either be typed in manually or browsed to.

The **Advanced** page provides some additional settings, including how SCEP treats archive files, whether the client will automatically scan removable drives and it also enables the creation of system restore points before taking action on a detected piece of malware. You can also grant the user the ablilty to view the malware incedent history and define how long items will be stored in the quarantine.

Although it might have a nefarious sounding name, **Spynet** is actually Microsoft's cloud-based service that allows SCEP clients to report information about programs that display suspicious behavior. The name Spynet is being phased out and rebranded as **Microsoft Active Protection Service** (**MAPS**). Keep in mind, on the local client side, the option is still called Spynet in the UI. Future service packs will most likely alleviate this discrepancy.

Spynet must be enabled if you plan on utlizing the **Dynamic Signature Service** component of SCEP. Dynamic Signatures are essentially cloud-based partial signatures files for new emerging threats, meaning these threats are so new that Microsoft has not had time to add these patterns to the latest version of the full SCEP definiton file.

Using Dynamic Signatures Service and enabling Spynet is especially recommended for clients that have higher than normal risk factors, such as "road warriors", who use their laptops from hotels, airports, and customer sites.

Utilizing MpCmdRun.exe

One of the most vital tools for a SCEP admin is `MpCmdRun.exe`. With this command-line utility, you can perform a definition rollback, force a signature update, restore a file from quarantine, or kick off a scan. Almost any operational scripting tasks you wish to perform will center on `MpCmdRun.exe`.

Getting Ready...

By default, `MpCmdRun` is stored in the `C:\Program Files\Microsoft Security Client\ Antimalware` directory. Although `MpCmdRun` can be used to accomplish many tasks with SCEP, this recipe will only describe how to launch a full scan from the command line.

How to do it...

1. Open the Command Prompt window.

2. Navigate to `C:\Program Files\Microsoft Security Client\Antimalware` directory.

3. Enter the following command:

   `MpCmdRun  -scan -2`

4. Once the full scan is completed, close the Command Prompt window.

How it works...

To view all options available for the utility, enter `MpCmdRun -?` in the Command Prompt window. A partial output is included for reference in the following example. The full contents of the `MpCmdRun` help file can be found in the appendix.

```
Usage:

MpCmdRun.exe [command] [-options]


Command Description
   -? / -h                                    Displays all available
options for this tool
   -Scan [-ScanType #] [-File <path> [-DisableRemediation]]  Scans for
malicious

   -Scan [-ScanType value]
        0   Default, according to your configuration
        1   Quick scan
        2   Full system scan
        3   File and directory custom scan


           [-File <path>]
```

There's more...

Below are some alternate examples of ways in which MpCmdRun could be utilized.

Using MpCmdRun to pull definition updates from an alternate source

One example of how MpCmdRun could be useful is a scenario where your WSUS infrastructure has gone offline and you want to temporarily force your clients to pull a definition from an alternate source without modifying the SCEP policy.

In this case, you would need to either manually enter the following command or create a script that contains the command:

```
MpCmdRun -signatureupdate -servername\sharename
```

Using MpCmdRun to de-quarantine a false positive

The `-restore` option can utilized to restore files that have been erroneously quarantined, without having to directly access the client UI. This could be done remotely using a tool such as **PsExec**.

MpCmdRun logging

MpCmdRun automatically creates a logfile called `MpCmdRun.log` in the directory `C:\Users\username\AppData\Local\Temp`. This logfile records any commands that are executed using `MpCmdRun.exe`.

2

Planning and Rolling Installation

In this chapter, we will cover:

- ▸ Creating role-based SCEP administrators
- ▸ Creating auto deployment rules for SCEP definitions
- ▸ Enabling the Endpoint Protection role

Introduction

With each version of its corporate antivirus solution, Microsoft has tried to tighten integration with their other core infrastructure products. Whereas, the previous release of Forefront Endpoint Protection needed to be installed on top of an SCCM 2007 infrastructure, SCEP is built into SCCM 2012 right out of the box. Once you've migrated from SCCM 2007 to SCCM 2012, utilizing SCEP in your environment requires little more than agreeing to an **End-user licence agreement** (**EULA**) and making sure you've got the licenses to cover your client base.

What requires for a little foresight and planning is making sure that the right staff members have access to SCEP's management tools within SCCM and that your organization's SCCM distribution points have up-to-date SCEP definitions preloaded. Providing your distribution points with definitions ahead of a SCEP deployment will help prevent a situation, where all of your newly deployed SCEP clients attempt to reach out over the Internet to Microsoft Updates, and pull a larger initial definition and engine package at the same time and thereby, saturate your WAN links.

The recipes in this section will help to accomplish both of these tasks.

Creating role-based SCEP administrators

One of the most talked about new features in SCCM 2012 is the ability to create **role-based administrators**. This feature allows you to easily grant a user a limited subset of administrative rights within SCCM that will allow them to perform their assigned tasks, but prevent them from doing anything beyond that.

SCCM 2012 includes an **Endpoint Protection Manager** role right out of the box.

This recipe will demonstrate how to add a user or group of users to this role.

The majority of the recipes in this book refer to tasks done on the **Central Administration Site** (**CAS**) server, which assumes that your organization has one. Smaller organizations may only have a single **primary site server**. If that is the case for you, then simply perform the task on your primary site server as if it was a CAS server.

Getting ready

To complete this task, you will need to have full administrative access to the SCCM 2012 console on the CAS in your SCCM infrastructure. While it is possible to extend this role to a single user, it's always recommended to grant permissions to a group of users instead.

How to do it...

Follow these steps:

1. Log into the CAS server and open **Configuration Manager Console**.
2. Navigate to the **Administration** workspace and open the **Security** object, and then select **Administrative Users**.

3. Click on the **Add User or Group** button in the menu bar at the top of screen. Next, in the **Add User or Group** window, click on **Browse** and locate a group in `Active` directory, as shown in the following screenshot:

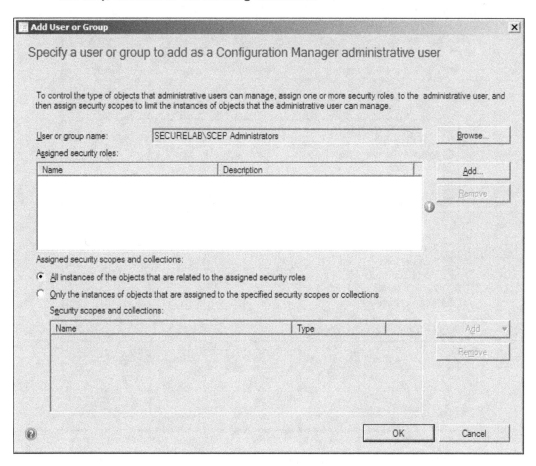

4. After the user or group has been populated in the **User or group name** field, click on the **Add...** button. The **Add Security Role** window should then pop up, select **Endpoint Protection Manager** from the list, and click on **OK**, as shown in the following screenshot:

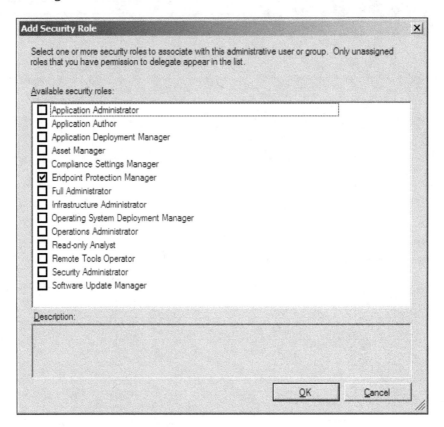

5. Once you've returned to the **Add User or Group** window, you now have the option to narrow the scope of where this role assignment will be applied by either selecting **All instances of the objects that are related to this security role** or choosing **Security scopes and collections** and selecting specific scopes and collections.

6. Clicking on **OK** will complete the process and return you to the SCCM management console.

How it works...

In SCCM 2012, security roles are used to quickly assign SCCM permissions to administrators that will allow them to perform a given task. In the case of the Endpoint Protection Manager role, a user will be granted the following permissions:

- Ability to define and monitor security policies
- Administrative users who are associated with this role can create, modify, and delete Endpoint Protection policies
- Ability to deploy Endpoint Protection policies to collect, create, and modify alerts and monitor Endpoint Protection status

In most cases, this should be sufficient for an administrator that had previously been assigned management tasks with a legacy anti-virus solution.

If the Endpoint Protection manager role should prove not to be comprehensive enough for the tasks that you'll be assigning to your AV administrators, it is possible to add additional permissions. To do this, it is suggested that you copy the role and grant the additional rights in the properties of the new custom role.

The same procedure can be used to remove permissions if the defaults prove to be too robust for your organization's security policies.

Creating auto deployment rules for SCEP definitions

Auto deployment rules are a new feature of SCCM 2012. Among other things, this feature was developed to optimize the deployment of definition updates while minimizing the impact on your network connections.

Previous versions of SCEP relied on either Microsoft Updates in the cloud, WSUS, or UNC file shares (all of which can still be used in SCEP) to push out definitions. The use of ADRs allows you to tap into your existing SCCM distribution points without the need for human interaction to keep them up-to-date.

Getting ready

The creation and management of automatic deployment rules is done within the **Software Updates Management** (**SUM**) component of SCCM 2012. Therefore, it is required that the SCCM server on which you are configuring these rules has the software update point installed.

In a large-scale hierarchical SCCM environment, this task would typically be conducted on the CAS.

How to do it...

Follow these steps:

1. Log into the CAS or connect to the CAS with your local SCCM console.

2. Select the **Software Library** workspace and expand **Software Updates** to locate the **Automatic Deployment Rules** container. Refer to the following screenshot:

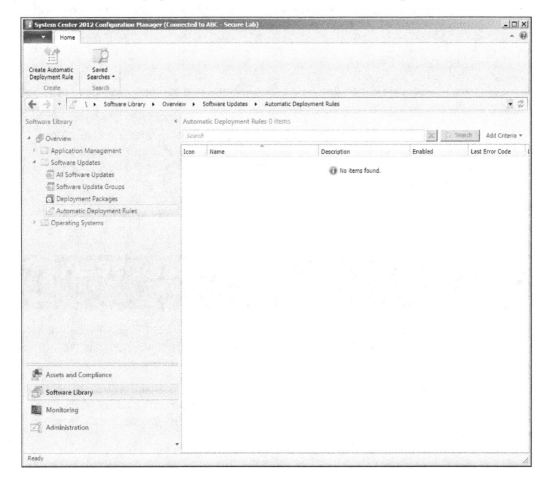

3. Click on **Create Automatic Deployment** rule in the upper left-hand side corner of the home ribbon to launch the **Create Automatic Deployment Rule Wizard** window.

4. On the **General** page, provide the rule with a name and select a collection to target. Verify that **Add to an existing Software Update Group** is selected, and then click on **Next** to proceed, as shown in the following screenshot:

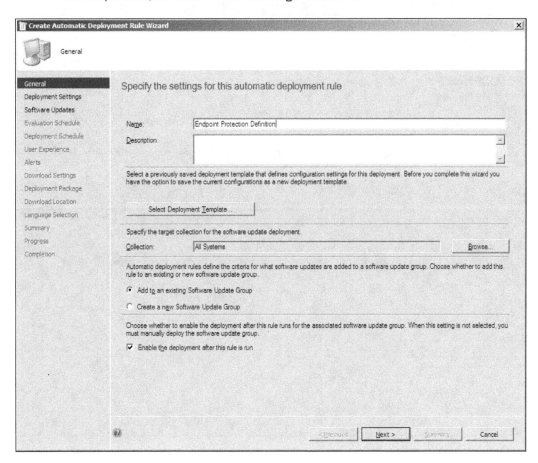

5. On the **Deployment Settings** page, set the detail level for state messages to **Minimal** and then click on **Next** to proceed.

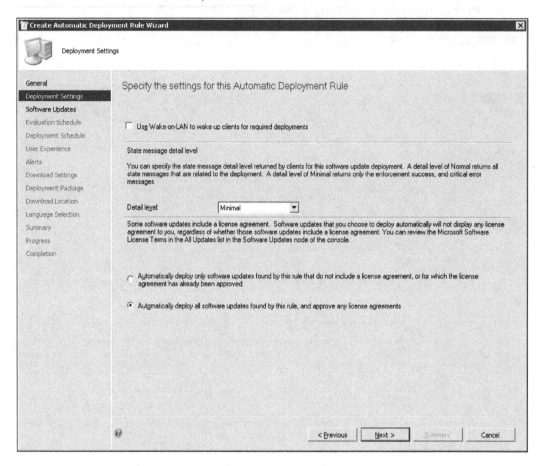

6. On the **Software Updates** page, select **Product** from the **Property filters** window and click on **<items to find>** in the **Search criteria** window below it.

7. The **Search Criteria** pop-up window should display, scroll through this, locate **System Center 2012 Endpoint Protection**, and then click on **OK**.

8. Now scroll through the **Property filters** window again and select **Date Released or Revised**.

9. By clicking on **<values to find>**, the **Search Criteria** window should pop up. Select **Last 1 day** from the drop-down list and then click on **OK**.

10. Now select **Update Classification** from the **Property filters** list and click on **<items to find>** from the **Search Criteria** window.

11. A **Search Criteria** pop-up window should appear; select **Definition Updates** from the list and click on **OK**. Refer to the following screenshot:

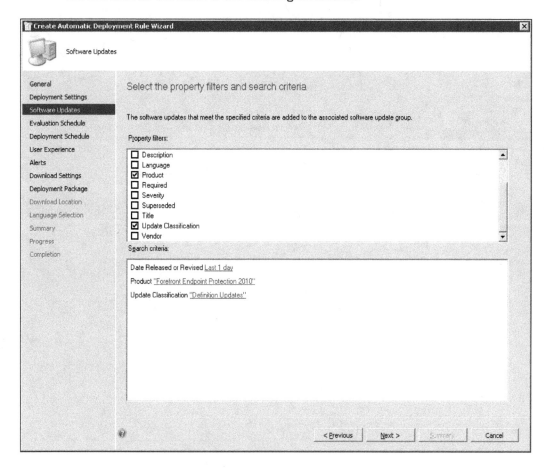

12. Click on **Next** to proceed to the **Evaluation Schedule** page, click the **Customize...** button, and change the default schedule to run once every day.

13. Clicking on **Next** will take you to the **Deployment Schedule** page.

14. In the **Software Available** field, select **Specific time**, then change the value to **2 Hours**.

15. Next, change the **Installation Deadline** to **Specific time** and change the value to **2 hours**. Refer to the following screenshot:

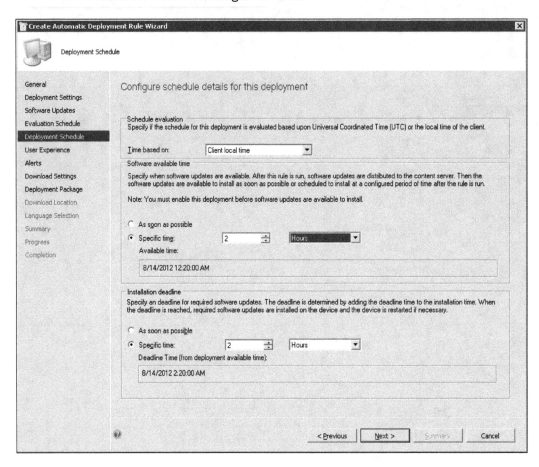

16. Click on **Next** to proceed to the **User Experience** page, make sure **Hide in Software Center and All Notifications** is selected from the **User notifications** drop-down list, and then click on **Nex**t to proceed. Refer to the following screenshot:

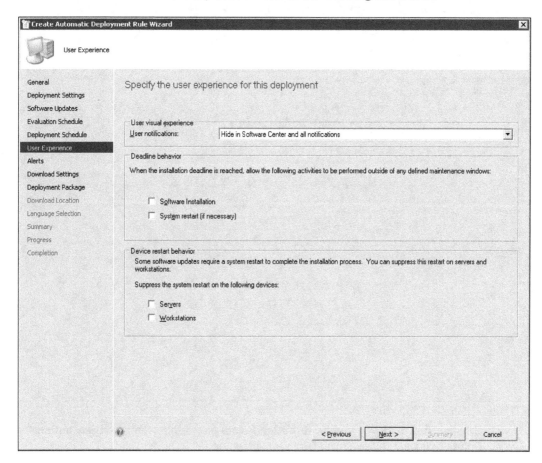

17. There is no need to deviate from the defaults on the **Alerts** page, so click on **Next** to proceed.

18. On the **Download Settings** page, select the **Download software updates from distribution point and install**, and then click on **Next** to move forward.

19. On the **Deployment Package** page, create a new package by first giving it a name.

20. Next, make sure to provide the wizard with a network path for the **Package source**. Refer to the following screenshot:

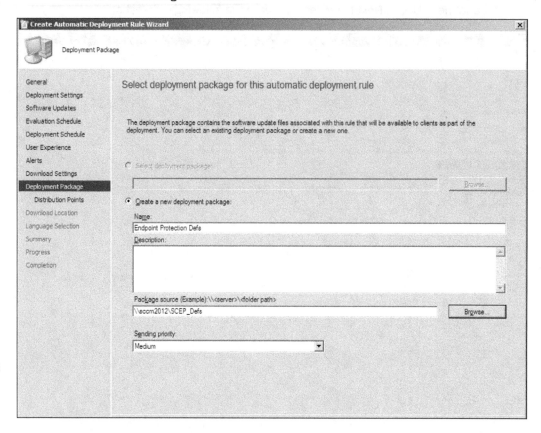

21. Click on **Next** to move to the **Distribution Points** page, and select the **Distribution Points** that want to have this ADR to replicate, too.

22. On the **Download Location** page, ensure that **Download software updates from the Internet** is selected, and click on **Next** to proceed.

23. On the **Language Selection** page, select the languages necessary for your organization.

24. Click on **Next** to view a summary; when ready, click on **Next** to have the rule created.

25. Once satisfied with the results, click on **Close** to end the wizard. The new rule will show up on the **Automatic Deployment Rules** panel in the SCCM console. Refer to the following screenshot:

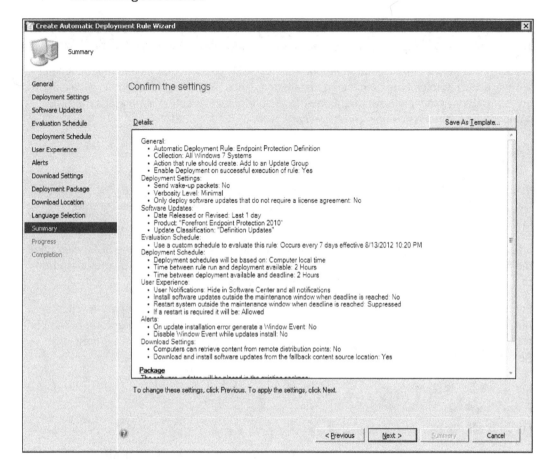

How it works...

The advantage of leveraging an **Auto Deployment Rule** (**ADR**) in advance of deploying the SCEP clients to your users, is that it will provide a nearby (in network terms) source for definitions to newly installed clients. The SCEP client software installs with no definitions whatsoever, so the very first definition package the client installs is critically important for security, as well as rather large in size (70 to 80 MB).

If a newly installed SCEP client cannot find a definition from a local source, it will eventually try and reach out to Microsoft Updates on the Internet. This is not a concern if you've only deployed SCEP to handful of systems; but if you've been planning on deploying to a couple of thousand PCs overnight, you can imagine what these thirsty clients might do to your WAN connections if they don't have a readily available source for definitions.

One important thing to note is that it is safe to apply a SCEP definition's ADR to a collection of systems that does not yet have SCEP installed; in this case, the ADR would simply be ignored by the client systems.

Enabling the Endpoint Protection role

Installing the server infrastructure components for SCEP could not be easier. In fact, it's not entirely accurate to call the process an installation, since all the bits for SCEP already exist on your CAS or primary site servers. Enabling the Endpoint Protection simply flips the SCEP components to the on position and takes care of the EULA for SCEP.

Getting ready

In order to complete the process for enabling SCEP, you will need to utilize a user account with the Full Administrator security role applied. If your account has only been granted the Endpoint Protection Manager role, this will not be sufficient for this process.

Also, keep in mind that part of this installation process is to install a baseline SCEP client on the SCCM servers themselves. This is necessary for the extrapolation of virus metadata from the local client's definitions to use in SCEP reports and alerts.

For the most part, the SCEP installation process is very good at removing legacy AV clients, but if your current AV solution has a password protection policy or some other form of tamper proofing, it's recommended that you disable that before starting the Endpoint Protection Role installation.

How to do it...

Follow these steps:

1. Log into the CAS server and open the **Configuration Manager Console**.

2. Navigate to the **Administration** workspace, and then drill down to **Site Configuration/Servers and Site System Roles**. Refer to the following screenshot:

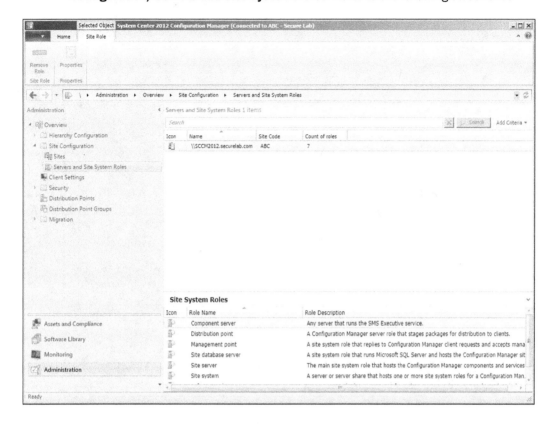

3. Right-click on your CAS server (or Primary Site server if you don't have a CAS) and select **Add Site System Roles**.

4. Verify whether all the auto populated values are correct on the **General** page, then click **Next** to proceed.

5. On the **System Role Selection** page, enable the check box next to **Endpoint protection point**, and click **Next** to move forward.

6. You should now see an EULA for SCEP; check the box to accept, and click on **Next** to proceed.

7. The next page sets the enterprise-wide default value for the level of participation in **Microsoft's Active Protection Service** (formerly known as Spynet). Make your selection and click **Next** to move to the summary page.

8. Once satisfied with the summary, click on **Next>** to initiate the installation process.

9. After the installation completes, you will be presented with a results page on the **Completion** screen, as shown in the following screenshot:

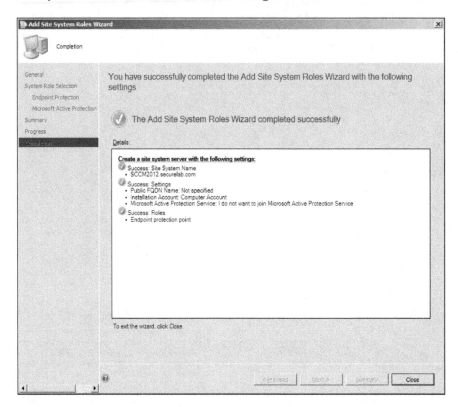

How it works...

Microsoft designed SCEP from the ground up to be seamlessly integrated with SCCM 2012. But, it's necessary to have a process where an organization must agree to an EULA.

Once the role has been installed, the **Endpoint Protection Manager Security role** should suffice for any future SCEP related activities.

The Active Protection Service:

Microsoft's Active Protection Service is a communication channel built into the SCEP client software that allows for automatic transmission of virus telemetry data back to Microsoft analysts at the Microsoft Malware Protection centre.

The two key benefits that come from participation in the Microsoft Active Protection Service are first that it is necessary for the dynamic definitions feature of SCEP to function, and second, it will help expedite the process of getting a previously unknown threat detected on one of your systems added to SCEP definitions.

3
SCEP Configuration

In this chapter, we will cover:

- ▶ Modifying SCEP default client settings
- ▶ Creating, modifying, and deploying an SCEP policy
- ▶ Setting up SCEP alerts
- ▶ Configuring reports

Introduction

So, now that you've successfully installed the Endpoint Protection Management role, let's focus our attention on some vital post-installation configuration tasks. In this chapter, we will be creating SCEP policies for your workstations and servers, as well as putting into place the system that will undoubtedly be responsible for alerting you in the middle of the night at some point in the future.

Modifying SCEP default client settings

The title of this section refers to an SCCM client's default settings that pertain to SCEP. These settings cover things, such as the installation of SCEP clients, and whether the existing AV client will be removed to make way for SCEP. Keep in mind, this is different from your default SCEP policy, which controls things such as scan times and custom exclusions.

One important thing to remember is that the baseline **Default Client Settings** policy will be enforced on every system in your SCCM environment, so exercise caution when modifying this policy. Let's say, for example, that you were to change the **Install Endpoint Protection client on client computers** setting to **True**. This would result in SCEP being automatically installed on every computer on your network with an SCCM 2012 client. For this reason, this recipe will walk you through the process of creating a Custom Client Device Settings policy and enforcing it on a collection for just a subset of your systems.

Getting ready

To complete this recipe, you will need a user account with full SCCM administration privileges. Default Client Settings do not fall under the purview of the Endpoint Protection Administrator role assignment. If your intention is to deploy SCEP to a limited number of test systems, it is recommended that you create a custom collection containing the target systems before going through this recipe.

How to do it...

Follow these steps:

1. Log into the CAS server and open the **Configuration Manager Console**.

2. Navigate to the **Administration** workspace, open the **Client Settings** object, and click on the **Create Custom Client Device Settings** button at the top left-hand side of the user interface. The **Create Custom Client Device Settings** window should appear like the following screenshot:

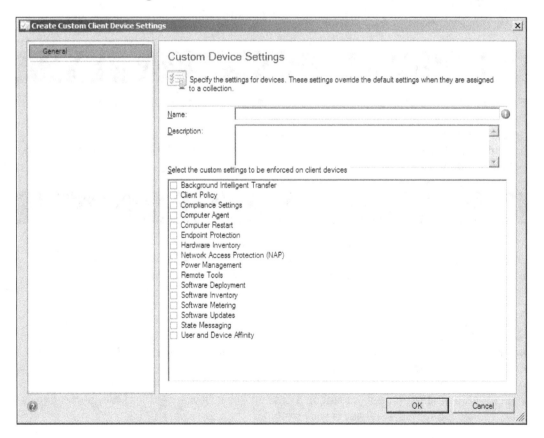

3. To begin modifying the policy, provide a **Name** and **Description**, then select **Endpoint Protection** from the list of options, and then select **Endpoint Protection** from the column on the left-hand side pane.

4. You should now be able to view the **Custom Device Settings** window for **Endpoint Protection**. Change the **Manage Endpoint Protection client on client computers** setting to **True**. Refer to the following screenshot:

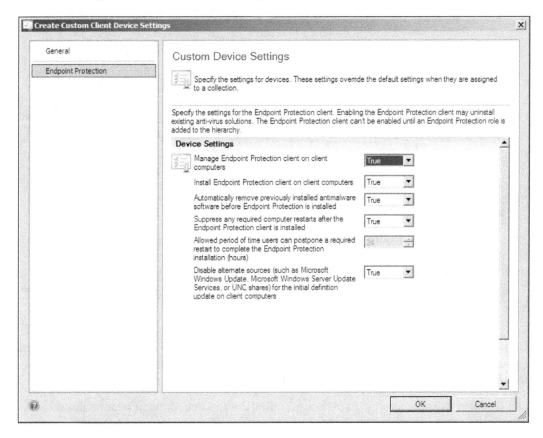

5. Leave the other settings as they are and click on **OK** to close the wizard. The **Custom Device Settings** policy you just created should now be viewable beneath the original **Default Client Settings** policy.

6. Right-click on the new policy that you created and select **Deploy**. From the list of collections, select the collection to which you want this policy to apply and click on **OK**. Refer to the following screenshot:

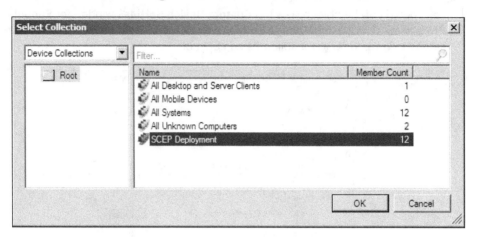

How it works...

The settings we've been modifying in this recipe are all related to the deployment of the SCEP client and will take effect whenever a computer is migrated from SCCM 2007 to SCCM 2012, or when the SCCM client is installed for the first time. It's important to note that deployment of the SCEP client is very different procedurally from previous versions. Any system that receives the SCCM 2012 client will receive the installation media or bits for SCEP, which are bundled with the SCCM client.

Modifying the **Custom Device Settings** option for **Install Endpoint Protection client on client computers** to **True** basically equates to flipping a switch on the target computer to use the installation media it already has.

The option for **Disable alternate sources for initial definition update on client computers** directly addresses an issue with deploying FEPs (the previous version) client to a large mass of computers simultaneously that could cause network saturation. This was caused by many clients reaching out to any available source to get their initial definition file (which is very large in size, 70 to 80 MB) at the same time. This setting will force all your new clients to get their first definition file as an SCCM package, thereby allowing you to control the flow of data and leverage all of SCCM's package delivery capabilities.

Just make sure that if you're going to make use of this option, you have set up a definition delivery package ahead of time (which is covered in _Chapter 2, Planning and rolling information_, of this book). Otherwise, you could have freshly-installed SCEP clients sitting out there with no definitions and therefore, unprotected.

Creating, modifying, and deploying a SCEP policy

The creation of anti-virus policies is probably the most critical task that any AV administrator is charged with. If the policy is too restrictive, then computers, and in turn, the end users, will be negatively impacted. Conversely, if the AV policy is too lenient, your computers will have an increased risk of becoming infected by malware.

Fortunately, SCEP provides many tools to make this constant balancing act a little easier for administrators. This recipe will guide you through the process of creating and modifying a SCEP policy for an average laptop user, who works with both while connected to the corporate and remote networks respectively.

The policy presented in this recipe is meant to serve as a reference, although the level of protection it offers is balanced with a minimal impact on the client PC, it should not be taken as list of best practice settings for every organization. Your corporate security standards may dictate that you adhere to a different level of protection.

Getting ready

To complete this recipe, you will need a user account with at least SCEP administrator role privileges.

How to do it...

Follow these steps:

1. Log into the CAS server and open the **Configuration Manager Console**.

2. Navigate to the **Assets and Compliance** workspace, open the **Endpoint Protection** object, and select **Antimalware Polices**. At the top left-hand side of the user interface, there is a button that reads **Create Antimalware Policy**; select it to launch the policy creation wizard. Refer to the following screenshot:

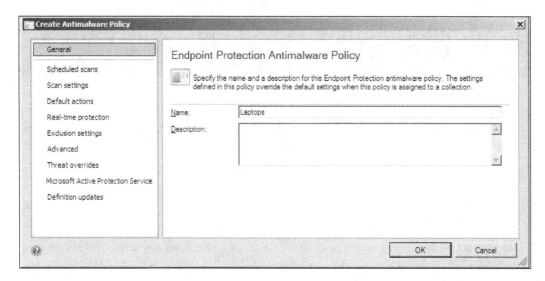

3. Begin by giving the policy **Name** and **Description**, then select **Scheduled scans** from the left-hand side column.

4. Change the **Scan Type** option from **Quick scan** to **Full scan**, and then change the **Limit CPU usage during scan to (%)** option to **30**.

5. Click **Scan settings** in the left-hand side column and change the settings for both **Scan email and email attachments** and **Scan removable storage devices such as USB drives** from **False** to **True**.

6. Next, click **Advanced** from the left-hand column and change the setting for **Show notification messages** from **False** to **True**.

7. Select **Microsoft Active Protection Service** from the left-hand side column and change the **Microsoft Active Protection Service membership** type option from **I do not want to join** to **Basic Membership**.

8. Now, select **Definition Updates** from the left-hand side and click on the button labeled **Select Source**, after which the **Configure Definition Update Sources** window should appear.

9. Make sure that **Updates distributed from Configuration Manager** and **Updates distributed from Microsoft Update** are both selected. Click on **OK** to close the window, as shown in the following screenshot:

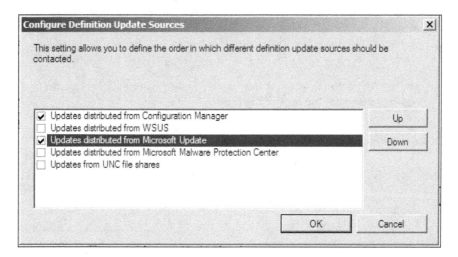

10. To deploy the policy, right-click on the policy you just created and select **Deploy.**

11. The **Select Collection** window should pop up; choose the collection to which you wish to apply this policy and click on **OK**.

How it works...

SCEP policies play a vital role in ensuring that your SCEP clients are both effectively protecting your systems from malware and, at the same time, maintaining an optimal level of performance. One of the biggest advantages to having an anti-malware solution that's tightly integrated with SCCM is that it allows you to effortlessly manage the deployment of AV polices. Once you've built a policy and deployed it to a collection, you can be certain that all the systems in that collection will receive the policy in short order.

There's More...

In addition to the aspects of SCEP policies that are discussed in the recipe, below is some additional information on SCEP policies that will be useful to you.

Understanding policy precedence

As an SCEP client will undoubtedly be a member of multiple collections within SCCM and you may have different SCEP policies assigned to these collections, it is necessary to implement a system of **policy precedence**. SCEP policy precedence can be modified by navigating to `Assets and Compliance\Overview\Endpoint Protection\Antimalware Policies` and right-clicking on a policy to either increase or decrease its priority.

 Remember that lower the number assigned in the **Order** column, the higher the rank of the policy.

Refer to the following screenshot:

Server policy templates

One of the most beloved features of the previous version of SCEP (Forefront Endpoint Protection) was the use of server policy templates. Microsoft wisely adapted all of its best practices for OS-level anti-virus running on its major application servers (Exchange, SQL, SharePoint, and so on) into a set of preconfigured FEP policies that you could select from a simple drop-down menu.

At first glance, it might seem as if this feature has been removed in SCEP, but while the process is no longer as simple as selecting a preset policy from a drop-down menu, the policy templates for servers are still included with SCEP.

To utilize them, simply click on the **Import** button at the top of the screen in the `Assets and Compliance\Overview\Endpoint Protection\Antimalware Polices`. It should automatically take you to the folder location where policy templates are stored. If you do not see the list of policy template XML files, navigate to `%instaldir%\Microsoft Configuration Manager\AdminConsole\XmlStorage\EPTemplates`; this is their default folder location.

Setting up SCEP alerts

Although every anti-virus administrator dreads the sound of a dozen alerts hitting their smartphone in the middle of the night, alerts are a necessary evil. The trick is to configure an alerts policy that correctly notifies you with actionable information, but does not inundate your administrators with a glut of unnecessary e-mails.

This recipe will walk you through the process of creating a set of SCEP alerts that will only notify you when an administrator's attention is necessary.

Getting ready

To complete this recipe, you will need to have access to a user account that has Full Administrator rights to the SCCM 2012 console. Alerts in SCEP are based on the membership of collections, so if you wish to create an alerts policy for a specific set of computers, it is advisable that you create this collection ahead of time.

Alerts are delivered via e-mail and they require an available Exchange SMTP resource; you will need to know the FQDN for the SMTP server in your environment.

How to do it...

Follow these steps:

1. Log into the CAS server and open the **Configuration Manager Console**. Navigate to `Assets and Compliance\Overview\Device Collections`, right-click on the collection you're targeting for this alerts policy, and select **Properties**.

2. Select the **Alerts** tab and check the box next to **View this collection in the Endpoint Protection dashboard**.

3. Click on the **Add...** button and the **Add New Collection Alerts** window should pop up. Now check the bottom four selections, and click on **OK**, as shown in the following screenshot:

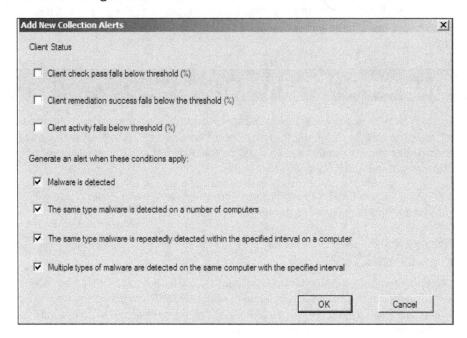

4. **Malware detection, Malware outbreak, Repeated malware detection**, and **Multiple malware detection** should now all appear in the **Conditions** window.

5. Select **Malware detection** and change the **Malware detection threshold** setting from **High** to **Medium – Detected, pending**.

6. Select **Multiple malware detection** from the **Conditions** window and change the **Number of malware types detected** from **2** to **4**. Then, click on **OK** to close the wizard.

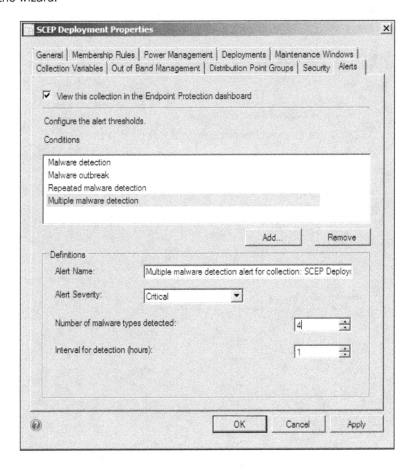

7. In order to receive these alerts over e-mail, you will need to configure the SMTP settings for the SCCM server. Navigate to `Administration\Overview\Site configuration` and right-click on the **Configure Site Components** button. Select **Email Notification** from the drop-down menu.

8. The **Email Notification Component Properties** window should pop up. Check the
    Enable email notification for Endpoint Protection alerts option and enter your
    Exchange server's FDQN. Specify an account to use for SMTP relay if it's required by
    your Exchange configuration, and provide **Sender address for email alerts** in the field
    provided. Refer to the following screenshot:

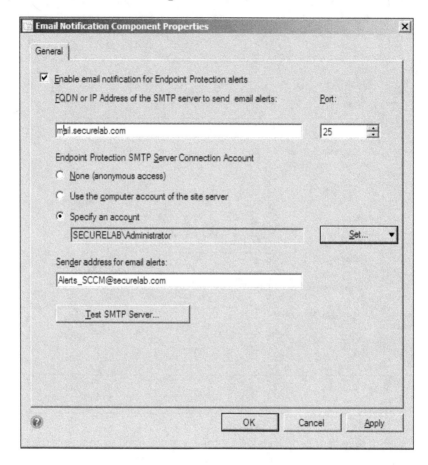

9. If you wish to conduct a test of these settings, click on the **Test SMTP Server** button.

10. The final piece to configuring alerts is to add e-mail addresses for users or distribute groups for the subscriptions of each alert type. To do this, navigate to `Monitoring\Overview\Alerts`, click on **Create Subscription**, and enable all of the different categories that you want to receive alerts for, as shown in the following screenshot:

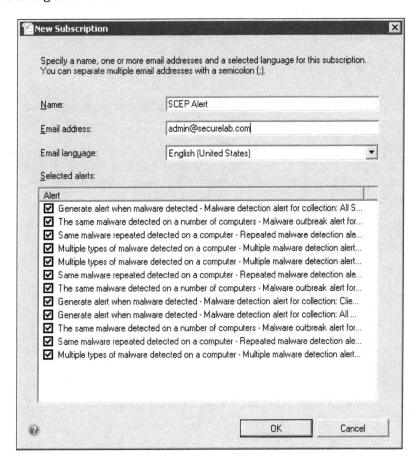

11. Click on **OK** to complete the wizard.

How it works...

Alerts in SCEP are handled by the SCCM 2012 infrastructure; they are assigned to collections of computers and have adjustable thresholds. This allows you to set up different collections with different levels of alerting. You could, for example, assign a high threshold to general workstation population, and a lower set of thresholds to critical servers.

Once alerts have been set up, you can tune them as needed if your administrators are getting either too few or too many e-mails from SCEP.

Configuring reports

While alerts allow for reactive responses to malware events, setting up a good reporting methodology will allow your administrators to be proactive in malware prevention efforts.

This recipe will walk you through the process of locating your SCEP reports and setting up your anti-malware activity report to be delivered on a scheduled basis via e-mail.

Getting ready

To complete this recipe, you will need to have access to a user account with at least the Endpoint Protection Manager security role.

If you wish to have your reports delivered via e-mail, it's required that the SQL reporting server hosting your reports has been configured to deliver reports via e-mail. If this has not yet been done, changing the e-mail settings on your SQL Reporting server will require SQL administrator rights.

How to do it...

Follow these steps:

1. Log into the CAS server and open the **Configuration Manager Console**.

2. Navigate to `Monitoring\Overview\Reporting\Reports` and locate your SCEP reports. If you've logged in with an account that only has the Endpoint Protection Manager role, these will be the only reports you're able to view. If you've logged in with a full administrator account, you can quickly filter the long list of available reports by entering the word `Endpoint` in the search field. Refer to the following screenshot:

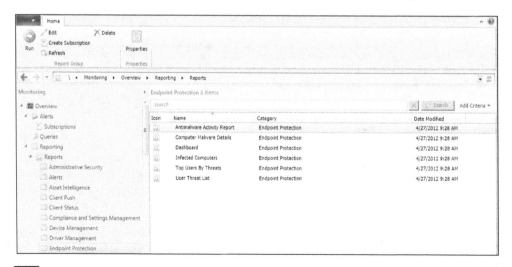

3. Right-click on the **Antimalware Activity Report** and select **Create Subscription**; change the **Report delivered by** option from **Windows File Share** to **Email**.

4. In the **To:** field, enter an e-mail address; this can be either a single user or a distribution group.

5. In the **Subject** field, provide a description of the report and make sure to check the box next to **Include Report**. The format you select for delivery is up to you, but I would recommend PDF, as it's readable on smartphones. All of the other settings are optional; click on **Next** to proceed. Refer to the following screenshot:

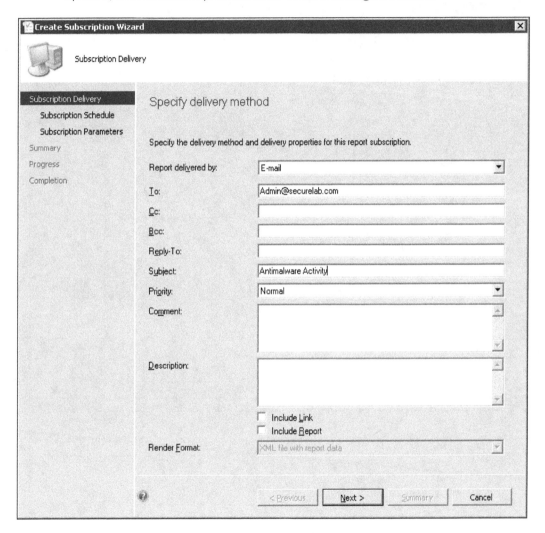

6. Next, set up the report delivery schedule and click on **Next** to proceed, as shown in the following screenshot:

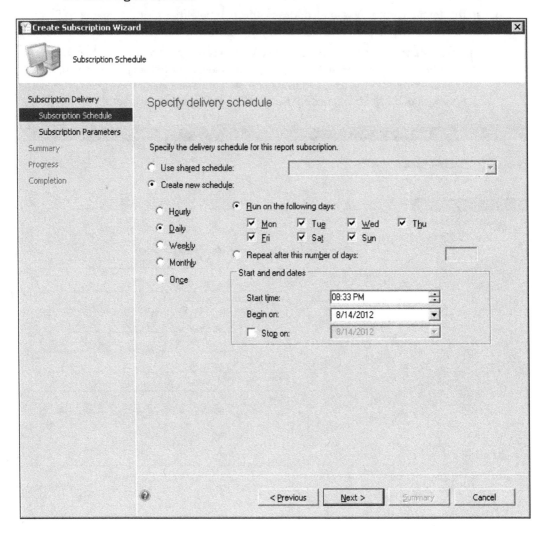

7. On the **Specify report parameters** page, you'll be required to select an SCCM collection that you want this report to be executed against. Click on **Next** to proceed, as shown in the following screenshot:

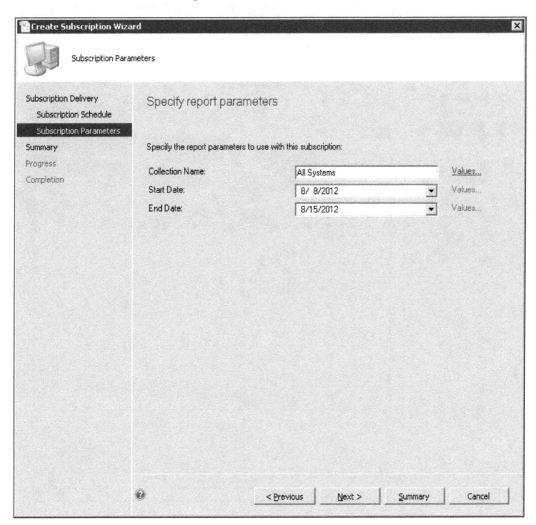

8. Review the settings you've chosen on the **Summary** page and click on **Next** to proceed, as shown in the following screenshot:

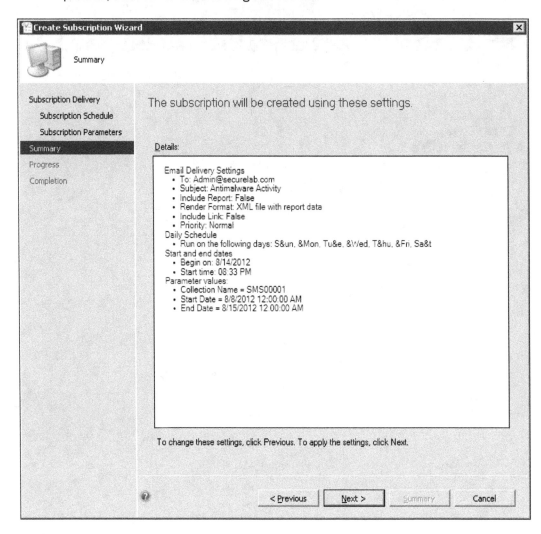

9. The wizard will create the report, and then display a completion message once it is done.

How it works...

SCEP utilizes SQL Reporting Services to run and deliver reports. Unlike previous iterations of the product, SCEP does not store anti-malware data in a separate data warehouse database. In SCEP, all anti-malware is stored directly in the configuration manager database. This allows for less administrative overhead and improves the speed at which virus related events are reflected in reports.

There's More...

Below are some other aspects of SCEP reporting that may be useful for you to understand.

Accessing reports without the SCCM console

The majority of users who will be working with SCEP will access reports by launching them from the SCCM console. You may, however, have some users that you wish to grant access to SCEP reports without granting access to the SCCM console. To accommodate these users, you can direct them to the URL for your SQL reporting server that is responsible for hosting your SCEP reports.

To begin, browse to the URL `http://yourSQLreportingservername/reports` and drill down to `configmgr_abc` (abc representing your own SCCM server's site code). In this directory, you should be able to see a directory named `Endpoint Protection`.

To grant a user access to this directory, select the **Security** tab and select **New Role Assignment**. Once this is done, the user should be able to navigate to the reports URL within Internet Explorer.

Delivering reports to smartphone users

As Malware events can happen at any hour of the day, it's advisable to configure your reports to be readable on any smartphone. In most cases, the best format for this is PDF, as nearly all major types of smartphones on the market today can open a `.pdf` file.

To accomplish this, select **Acrobat (PDF) file** as the **Render Format:** on the first page of **Create Subscription Wizard**. This will allow a user on a smartphone to fully read the report even if their device is not connected to your corporate network via VPN.

4
Client Deployment Preparation and Deployment

In this chapter, we will cover:

- ▸ Preparing your environment for SCEP
- ▸ Creating an effective deployment plan
- ▸ Deploying SCEP clients with SCCM 2012
- ▸ Verifying that SCEP policies are being applied correctly
- ▸ Performing a manual SCEP client installation

Introduction

Once you've completed your installation and basic configuration of the SCEP role on your SCCM 2012 server, it's time to start thinking about how you're going to roll the SCEP client out to your user base. Microsoft has done a fantastic job of making SCEP client deployment a quick and easy task.

Maybe, it's even a bit too easy in some regards. In the most basic term, an anti-virus client is software that will be installed on every Windows-based computer in your environment and will have a direct effect on the performance of every piece of software that is allowed to run on your PCs. Not to mention, it is the last line of defense in your anti-malware strategy.

So it's always best practice to do a little preparation and planning before actually pulling the trigger on your roll out.

Once the installation and configuration of your SCEP infrastructure is completed and you've gone through the deployment planning process, you'll be ready for the main event in a SCEP implementation, that is, client deployment.

This chapter contains recipes that will help to make this task considerably easier. You'll be learning how to initiate a client deployment in a phased and controlled manner, as well as how to monitor the progression of your deployment. You'll also be learning how to deploy the client manually without the use of SCCM and what to do if your newly installed SCEP clients have any issues receiving updates or communicating their status back to the SCCM environment.

Preparing your environment for SCEP

SCEP works on a wide range of Microsoft operating systems and almost any flavor of Windows run by a modernized organization. The quick rule of thumb is: if the system can handle an SCCM 2012 client (Windows XP SP2 for x64 and SP3 for x86, or above), it can run the SCEP client. It is essential to identify any legacy systems that will not support SCEP and plan accordingly.

Although SCEP does a great job of removing a competitive AV client before it installs itself, it's a good idea to make sure that your current AV is not going to impede the installation of SCEP in any way.

This recipe contains a series of questions that will assist you in determining your level of preparedness before deploying SCEP. As mentioned in *Chapter 2, Planning and Rolling Installation*, if your systems already have an SCCM 2012 client installed, then they already have the installation media for SCEP on their hard drive. What we are preparing to do here is, effectively, just flipping the switch on the install.

Getting ready

To complete this recipe, you should be familiar with your current AV and its policy configuration. In remediating any shortcomings that you may identify, you will likely need administrator level access to your current AV's management console and SCCM.

How to do it...

By working through each of the following items, important preparation tasks will be identified:

1. Do the workstations to which you are deploying SCEP have an SCCM 2012 client installed on them? If not, will they support an SCCM 2012 client?

2. Is your current AV solution one of the following?

    ❑ Symantec Endpoint Protection Planning and Rolling Installation Version 11

    ❑ Symantec Endpoint Protection Small Business Edition Version 12

    ❑ Symantec Corporate Edition Version 10

- ❏ McAfee Virus Scan Enterprise Version 8.5, Version 8.7, and its agent
- ❏ Forefront Client Security Version 1 and the Operations Manager agent
- ❏ Trend Micro Office Scan Version 8 and Version 10
- ❏ All current Microsoft anti-malware products except for Windows Intune and Microsoft Security Essentials
- ❏ If not, reach out to your vendor's technical support to acquire an uninstallation tool

3. If the current AV is one of the products that is supported for automatic removal, does your current policy enforce tamper proofing? For example, Symantec can require a password for uninstallation, or McAfee EPO can enforce reinstallation if its client is removed.

4. Are you utilizing a Firewall provided by your current AV vendor?

How it works...

The items in the preceding recipe are designed to help you identify any potential pitfalls to a successful SCEP deployment.

The first item is meant for you to consider the proliferation of SCCM 2012 to your deployment targets. It's okay to deploy the SCCM 2012 client software and SCEP at the same time. The thing to consider is that if a machine must support SCCM 2012 to utilize SCEP, older systems, such as Windows 2000 and Windows XP SP 2 or below, will need to be either upgraded or phased out. If neither of these options is feasible, it is recommended that you reach out to your Microsoft sales person and acquire licenses for Forefront Client Security, the predecessor to FEP and SCEP. FCS is still supported (as of the writing of this book) and will work on most legacy systems.

If your current AV is one of the products listed in second item, then your removal procedures will be a snap. If not, it's going to be more difficult. The best thing to do is reach out to your current vendor and ask for a removal tool (VBS script, EXE, bat file, and so on). They should have such a tool to share with you, though keep in mind that for security purposes, vendors typically don't make removal tools available through their website. Once you've got the tool, you should run some trials to ensure its effectiveness. If it functions as advertised, you'll need to build a custom SCEP deployment method, which will be discussed later in the book.

Most corporate AV solutions have some kind of tamper protection to keep users or malicious processes from removing it easily. You'll want to make sure these protections are lifted before deploying SCEP. A good best practice is to remove tamper protection for only a subset of computers to which you're planning to deploy SCEP in the near future, rather than lifting the tamper protection for every PC in your company all at once.

The fourth item asks if you are currently using an Endpoint firewall that is part of your overall anti-virus solution. SCEP is designed to utilize the **Windows Firewall with Advanced Security**. If you are using a Firewall solution from Symantec, for example, you will need to plan on implementing the Windows Firewall to replace its functionality. Any custom exclusion you've made to the Symantec Endpoint Firewall would need to be added to the Windows Firewall policy. The best way to administer your Windows Firewalls is through **Group Policy Objects**.

Creating an effective deployment plan

As you move through these recipes, you're moving closer and closer to initiating an enterprise-wide SCEP deployment. Don't be scared, if you take the time to really think through the items in this recipe, you'll be setting yourself up for a pretty painless deployment.

Getting ready

To answer the following items, you will need to have a good understanding of your corporate network as a whole. If you were not a part of the initial SCCM 2012 design, you may need to reach out to your SCCM administrators to verify answers for some of the following items.

How to do it...

Working through the following items will walk you through the process of preparing your environment for SCEP:

1. Has your SCCM 2012 been scaled out to support the number of SCEP clients you are intending to deploy?

2. Have you implemented enough distribution points to supply SCEP definitions on a daily basis without affecting network performance?

3. Have you disseminated enough information about the upcoming deployment to technical staff and end users?

4. Have you fully tested your legacy AV removal procedure? If not absolutely 100 percent effective on all of your test clients, what is the expected percentage of failure?

5. Have you created a procedure for dealing with failed SCEP installations?

6. Have you created and tested SCEP policies for all the system types that your deployment targets?

7. Is there an existing channel of communication for end users that experience performance issues after SCEP is deployed?

8. Has there been a maintenance window created for deploying SCEP to Windows servers?

9. Is your help desk ready to respond to an increased number of virus detections?
10. Have you grouped your deployment targets into logical groups of systems that will allow for deploying in a phased manner?

How it works...

When considering the first item in this list, it's important to make sure that your SCCM 2012 environment is robust enough to support all of the SCEP clients you are intending to deploy. If your implementation of SCCM was in a pilot phase, make sure it's ready to support a production-wide deployment. Check to make sure there are enough primary sites and distribution points to cover your user base. Make sure good backup and disaster recovery procedures are in place.

The second item should have you thinking about placement of distribution points. A quick rule of thumb is that you don't want more than a handful of systems in a given site pulling updates over a WAN connection. If it's possible, plan to have a DP in each geographical site.

The importance of the third item, Have you disseminated enough information about the upcoming deployment to technical staff and end users?, should not be underestimated. With the proliferation of malware of the "fake" AV type, users have become increasingly savvy about what's in their system tray. It's a good idea to communicate with your end users about SCEP and what the icons should look like before initiating a deployment.

The fourth item, Have you fully tested your legacy AV removal procedure?, speaks to the reality of any production-wide deployment. No process is perfect, and when you're deploying something such as SCEP to every computer on your network, it's really a percentage game. It's better to be realistic about this and identify what you think the failure rate is going to be, and create a remediation plan to quickly deal with any clients that fail to install SCEP correctly. During your pilot phase, I would recommend deploying SCEP to a non-vital machine, without removing the legacy AV client. This will allow you to know what happens when both SCEP and the legacy AV are running on the same machine at the same time.

Because we're leveraging SCCM for deployment, the answer to the fifth item should be straightforward. Monitoring the success and failure of a SCEP advertisement is done within the SCCM console. If clients do fail to install SCEP, it's a good idea to have a manual SCEP installation procedure on hand.

The sixth item asks, Have you created and tested SCEP policies for all the system types that your deployment targets?. Remember that computers are grouped together logically by collection in SCEP. So if you've created, for example, an Exchange Server 2010 SCEP policy, you will need to have a collection of just Exchange 2010 Servers to which you apply this policy.

The seventh item asks if you've created a channel of communication between end users and the staff that are deploying SCEP. This is very important, as it will allow you to quickly address any performance issues by modifying SCEP policies as needed. That being said, try not to overreact to every user concern. The truth is, there are a lot of perception issues, where endpoint anti-virus is concerned. It's best to verify that an issue is really being caused by the SCEP client rather than create an abundance of unnecessary exclusions and exceptions.

The eighth item should get you thinking about your deployment plan for pushing SCEP to Windows servers. Usually, server operators will choose to manually install an AV client rather than automate the installation and run the risk of an unscheduled reboot. This is perfectly acceptable, however, just make sure that your operators fully understand the manual SCEP installation process and that your SCEP administrators follow up with confirming servers, which are showing up correctly in the SCEP dashboard. Manual installation procedures are covered later in this book.

The ninth item asks, Is your help desk ready to respond to an increased number of virus detections?. This should not be taken to mean that SCEP is going to cause your workstations to become infected. Quite the opposite, whenever an organization updates their AV to the new cutting-edge solution, it's normal to suddenly find infections that may have been going unnoticed. Just make sure your help desk staff is ready for this event, to avoid unnecessary panic.

The tenth item is meant to get you to think about how your computers are grouped together, either by geographical site or by their role. Stretching a deployment out over a period of time, maybe a couple of weeks, is always a better practice than trying to deploy to the entire organization overnight. This will ensure that the number of failed deployments is always small enough for your staff to respond in timely manner.

Deploying SCEP clients with SCCM 2012

One of the biggest differences between SCEP and its predecessor FEP is the way in which the clients are deployed. FEP clients were deployed using an SCCM 2007 software package and an advertisement. While the system of software packages and advertisements persists in SCCM 2012, it is not used at all to deploy SCEP clients.

Instead, Microsoft has bundled the SCEP client within the SCCM 2012 client. The SCCM client agent settings determine whether or not a client PC is running SCEP. Changing the Endpoint Protection settings in the options for Client Agents essentially amounts to flipping a switch that tells a targeted computer to go ahead and use the SCEP client it already has.

In previous versions of SCCM, it was possible to have one set of client agent settings; in SCCM 2012, you can now have multiple sets of client settings and limit them to a given collection. So rather than modifying the default client settings policy, and thereby, deploying SCEP to every system with an SCCM 2012 client, we will be using a custom client settings policy and limiting our initial SCEP deployment to a smaller subset of PCs.

This is commonly referred to as a pilot deployment. Limiting the number of PCs to which we initially deploy SCEP will help you verify your deployment plan and to identify any issues with SCEP running on your organization's computers. It is always a best practice for a pilot to select a group of workstations and servers that represent a good cross section of your organization's overall user base.

Getting ready

To complete this recipe, you will need to be using an account which has full SCCM admin privileges. It's also recommended that you've identified which PCs and servers will be in the pilot group and that you've placed them together in an SCCM collection.

How to do it...

Follow these steps:

1. Log into your SCCM CAS server and launch the SCCM 2012 management console.
2. Navigate to `Administration | Overview | Client Settings`.
3. Click on the **Create Custom Client Device Settings** button at the top of the interface.
4. The **Create Custom Client Device Settings** window will pop up; enter a **Name** and check the box next to **Endpoint Protection**, as shown in the following screenshot:

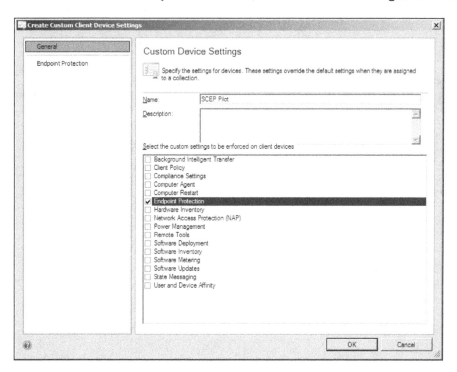

5. Next, select **Endpoint Protection** from the menu on the left-hand side. The screen displays all of the **Custom Device Settings** that apply to SCEP, as shown in the following screenshot:

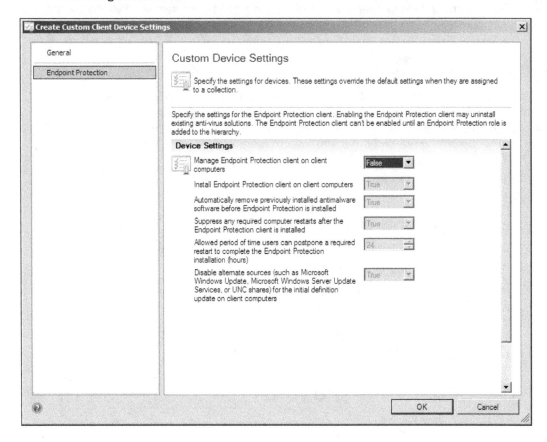

6. Change the value for **Manage Endpoint Protection client on client computers** from **False** to **True**.

7. This should cause all of the **True** or **False** options in this window to switch to **True**. If for some reason, this does not happen, set them all to **True** manually.

8. Click on **OK** to close the window, and your new custom client settings policy should be added to the list of client settings. Refer to the following screenshot:

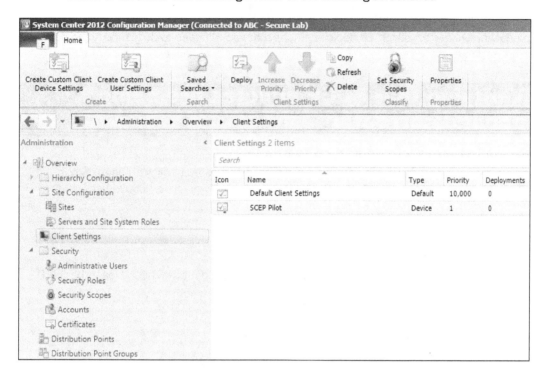

9. Now it's time to deploy the client settings policy that we just created. To do this, right-click on the new policy and select **Deploy**.

10. The **Select Collection** window will pop up. Search through the list of collections and find the collection you created for this pilot. Click on **OK** to close the window.

How it works...

As the default setting in the default client settings policy is **False** for the option to enable SCEP, you must either change this setting to **True** (which will take effect for every SCCM client on your network) or create a custom client settings policy that enables SCEP.

As client settings policies are cumulative, any settings you've customized in the default policy will also go into effect. Only PCs that are a part of the pilot systems collection will receive the additional settings you enabled in the custom policy. SCCM uses a system of precedence for client settings policies, in which the policies with a numerically lower value win out over client settings policies with higher numerical value for priority. The default client settings policy has a priority value of **10,000** and the new policy we created in this recipe has a value of **1**, meaning if there are any conflicting settings, the new custom policy gets its way.

As the installation media or bits for the SCEP client is bundled with the SCCM 2012 client, we will not need to push any other software to the systems in the pilot group.

If the pilot is successful (which I'm sure it will be), and you've made the decision to go production-wide with your SCEP deployment, all that you will need to do is modify the default client settings policies settings for SCEP just as we did in this recipe.

Verifying that SCEP policies are being applied correctly

One very important aspect of your SCEP deployment is to stay on top of which policy your clients are receiving. All new SCEP clients will receive the default policy automatically, but if you've added any additional SCEP policies with custom settings, it's a good idea to check and make sure that your clients have received the policy correctly.

Getting ready

In order to complete this recipe, you'll need to utilize an account that has at least the SCEP administrators SCCM role assigned to it.

How to do it...

Follow these steps:

1. Log into your SCCM CAS server and launch your SCCM 2012 management console.

2. Navigate to `Assets and Compliance | Overview | Devices` and locate the collection that the custom policy has been assigned to.

3. Select any of the systems in this collection, and then click on the **Endpoint Protection** tab at the bottom of the screen.

4. You should be able to see a column titled **Policy Application Information**. The first item under the title is called **EP Policy Name**, which is followed by the name of the current policy that is in effect for this client, as shown in the following screenshot:

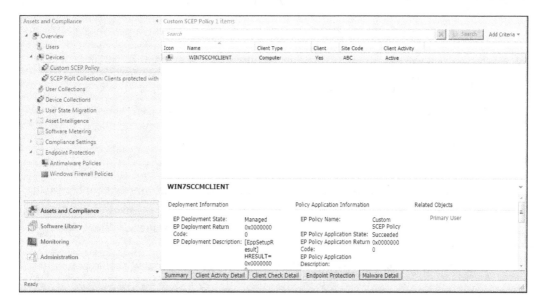

How it works...

SCEP clients receive their policy settings as SCCM advertisements of small XML files. Once a SCEP policy has been created, it needs to be assigned to an SCCM collection of computers to go into effect.

If you follow the preceding recipe and find that the computer you were spot-checking does not have the correct policy, go back to Assets and Compliance | Overview | Endpoint Protection | Antimalware Policies and double-check that your custom policy is assigned to the right collection.

If you've just deployed a new policy within the past few minutes and find that a computer does not have the correct policy, give it a few minutes and refresh the screen. It can take a while for a newly deployed policy to make its way down to a client.

Performing a manual FEP client installation

It is a fact that when working in a large corporate network environment, there will always be the oddball PC that, for whatever reason, cannot be joined to the domain or won't have the SCCM client installed. These could be lab machines, special purpose kiosk PCs, or controllers for manufacturing equipment.

Regardless of why these PCs needed to be orphaned, if they are running Windows, they still need an anti-virus client. This recipe will walk you through the process of putting together the installation media for this task and installing the FEP client manually on a single PC.

Getting ready

For this recipe, you will need to be utilizing an account that has at least the SCEP administrator role assignment attached to it. You will also need an account that has local administrator privileges for the PC on which you'll be installing the client.

How to do it...

Follow these steps:

1. Log into your SCCM CAS server and launch your SCCM 2012 management console.

2. Navigate to `Software Library | Overview | Application Management | Packages`, right-click on the object called **Configuration Manager Client Package**, and select **Properties**.

3. The **Configuration Manager Client Package Properties** window should pop up, select that tab titled **Data Source**, and locate the **Source Folder** field, as shown in the following screenshot:

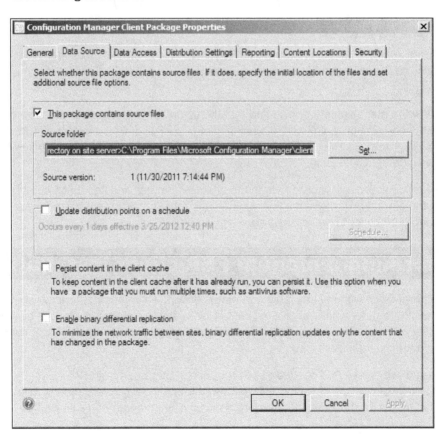

4. Make note of the path listed in the **Source Folder** field, then enter the same path into Windows Explorer. Once you've done this, you can click on **Cancel** to close the **Configuration Manager Client Package Properties** window.

5. The contents of the folder should be identical to the following screenshot:

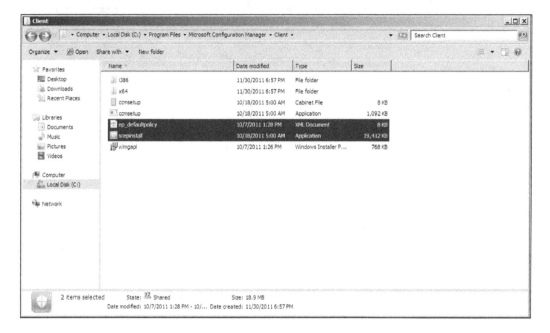

6. The only two files in this directory that we need right now are `ep_defaultpolicy.xml` and `scepinstall.exe`. Copy these two files to a thumb drive or a CD-R.

7. Now log in to the PC we're targeting for a manual SCEP installation and insert the media format.

8. Open a command prompt with admin privileges and enter the following syntax:

```
SCEPInstall.exe /policy C:\scep\ep_defaultpolicy.xml
```

In your case, the path for **ep_defaultpolicy** will be the installation media you have selected. Press *Enter* and the SCEP installer should pop up. Keep in mind that if you have modified your SCCM client install directory, the policy file will be in that customized directory. Refer to the following screenshot:

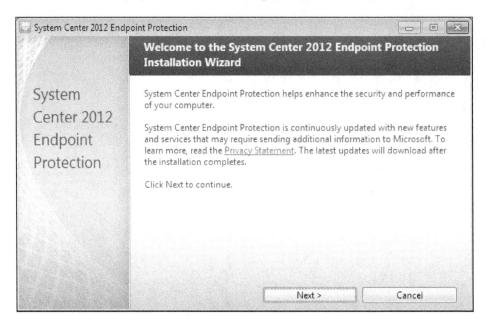

9. Proceed through the wizard, making your selections as you go. Once the wizard has completed, make sure that the SCEP client is able to download its initial set of definitions.

How it works...

The hardest part of this recipe is locating your SCEP client installation media, because the only copy you'll have is the one that's been bundled with the SCCM client installation package.

By copying both, the SCEP install.exe and the policy .xml file, and then running them manually on a target client, you'll end up with a SCEP client that starts off with a similar configuration to your normal SCCM-deployed SCEP clients.

Keep in mind that any future changes to this PC's SCEP policy will need to be done manually. Also, in order to get definition updates, this PC's SCEP client will either need to be able to reach Microsoft Updates on the Internet or a WSUS server in your environment that is enabled to push SCEP definitions.

It goes without saying that any anti-malware related events on this PC will not be reported to the SCCM server. So it will be up to the user of this PC to keep an eye on what's going on with the system; much like you would manage an AV client on your home computer.

5
Common Tasks

In this chapter, we will cover:

- ▶ Checking that your SCCM server has up-to-date SCEP definitions
- ▶ Performing SCEP operational tasks using the SCCM console
- ▶ Using SCEP reports to verify task completion
- ▶ Utilizing the SCEP dashboard
- ▶ Using MpCmdRun remotely

Introduction

In this chapter, we'll be covering operational SCEP tasks; in other words, the day-to-day procedures that any SCEP administrator will need to know how to perform. These recipes will show you how to make the most out of the SCEP management features that are built into the SCCM console. We'll also be showing you procedures that you may wish to build to document standards for reacting to a virus outbreak.

Overtime, these tasks will become second nature, and knowing how to perform them quickly will save you many headaches when a virus outbreak situation occurs.

Checking that your SCCM server has up-to-date SCEP definitions

It is no exaggeration to say that this task is the single most important thing that a SCEP admin does on a day-to-day basis. Keeping your SCCM CAS server's Software Update Point up-to-date with the newest SCEP definitions is the first link in the chain to get your SCEP clients the newest possible definitions.

Getting ready

In order to complete this recipe, you'll need to utilize an account that has at least the SCEP administrators SCCM role assigned to it.

How to do it...

Follow these steps:

1. Log into your SCCM CAS server and launch your SCCM 2012 management console.

2. Navigate to Software Library | Overview | Software Updates | All Software Updates.

3. In the **Search** bar, type the word Endpoint and press *Enter*, as shown in the following screenshot:

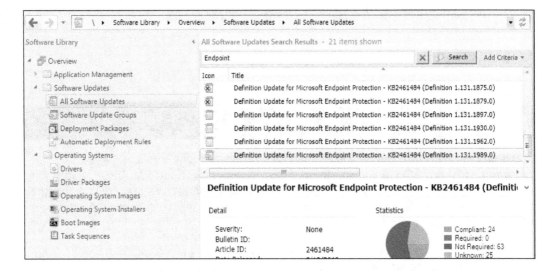

4. From the search results, select the item that ends in the highest numerical number; in this example that would be (**Definition 1.123.1813.0**). You can typically determine which version is the newest by looking for the title that has a green icon preceding it, as shown in the following screenshot:

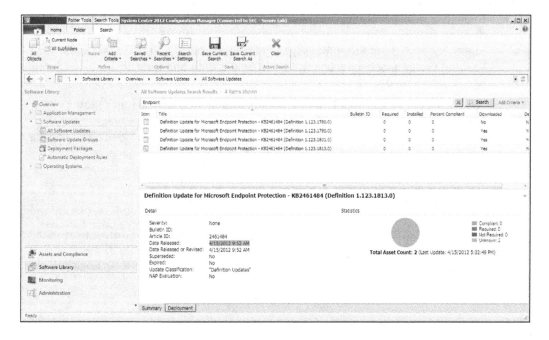

5. Now look for the **Date Released:** information on the bottom half of the console. If this date and time stamp is more than 8 hours in the past, you may not have the most up-to-date definition on your Software Update Point.

6. Click the **X** button at the end of the search bar to return to main window for Software Updates.

7. If you wish to force an unscheduled synchronization, click on the **Synchronize Software Updates** button in the top left-hand side corner of the console. Click on **Yes** on the information pop-up window to proceed, as shown in the following screenshot:

8. To check the status of the sync, navigate to `Monitoring | Overview | System Status | Component Status` and locate the **SMS_WSUS_Sync_Manager** item. Right-click and select **Show Messages**, then select **All**. The **Status Messages: Set Viewing Period** window will pop up. In the **Select date and time** field, choose **1 day ago** and click on **OK**.

9. You should be presented with a window titled **Configuration Manager Status Message Viewer for <SEC> <Secure Lab>**. If you see that top message in the window has **Message ID** of **6702**, then you know WSUS synchronization is complete. If **6702** is not the newest status message, then wait for a few minutes and refresh the screen by hitting *F5*.

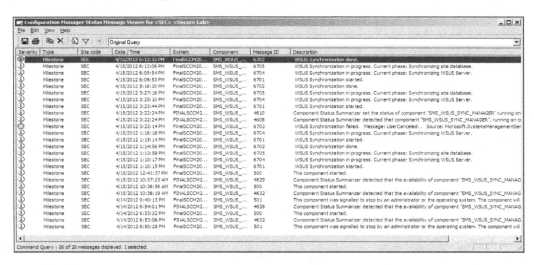

10. Once WSUS synchronization is complete, repeat steps 2 through 5 to see if the Software Update Component has a newer definition file than before. If so, proceed to step 11.

11. You will also want to manually execute your **Automatic Deployment Rule for SCEP** definitions, as the output of this rule is the package from which your SCEP clients actually get their definitions. To do this, navigate to `Software Library | Overview | Software Updates | Automatic Deployment Rules`, locate your rule for SCEP definitions, right-click, and select **Run Now**.

How it works...

The Software Updates component of your SCCM server uses Windows Server Update Services or WSUS to synchronize with Microsoft Updates over the Internet. It is important to remember that when you click on the **Synchronize Software Updates** button, SCCM will sync all of the available Microsoft Updates for all of the products it has been configured to receive in products and classifications.

On a normal day, this should usually just cause SCEP definitions to sync. However, if you manually kicked off a sync on **Patch Tuesday**, you may be pulling down a lot of data from Microsoft Updates. Unfortunately, there is no way to tell SCCM to only sync the SCEP definitions, and nothing else.

If everything is working correctly with SCCM, you will usually only need to follow step 1 through step 5, as everything else should be happening automatically on a regular basis. Steps 6 through step 11 are not something that you should need to do on a daily basis. If you do find yourself doing these steps routinely, then you should troubleshoot your SCCM server to determine why it is not syncing on its own.

Performing SCEP operational tasks using the SCCM console

When the term Operation Task is used in the context of an AV solution, it generally refers to something such as kicking off a non-scheduled quick or full scan, or perhaps forcing an out-of-band definition update. These are things you would likely be doing in response to malware detection or a malware outbreak.

Having a solid understanding of how these tasks can be accomplished within SCEP will help you to respond quickly to a developing situation.

This recipe has been written in accordance with a scenario in which an administrator is responding to a malware detection alert on a specific PC. For the purposes of this scenario, it is assumed that the administrator's corporate security policy dictates that any PC that has a malware detection alert has to receive an out-of-band definition update and must run a full scan.

Getting ready

To complete this recipe, you will need to be using an account that has at least the SCEP administrator role granted to it.

How to do it...

Follow these steps:

1. Log into your SCCM CAS server and launch the SCCM 2012 management console.
2. Type the name of the client system that you wish to target into the search bar and press *Enter*.

3. The target system should now be the only one in the list, as shown in the following screenshot:

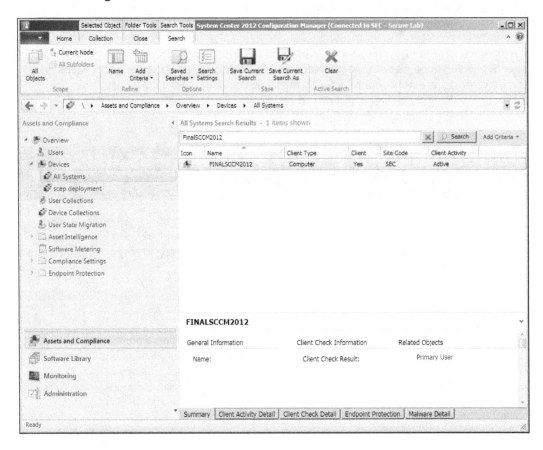

4. To review this PC's individual malware history, first select the PC from the list, and then click on **Malware Detail** at the bottom of the interface, as shown in the following screenshot:

5. To force an unscheduled definition update on this client, right-click on the PC name in the center of the interface. Select **Endpoint Protection**, and then left-click on **Download Definition**. Click on **OK** on the information pop-up window to complete this step, as shown in the following screenshot:

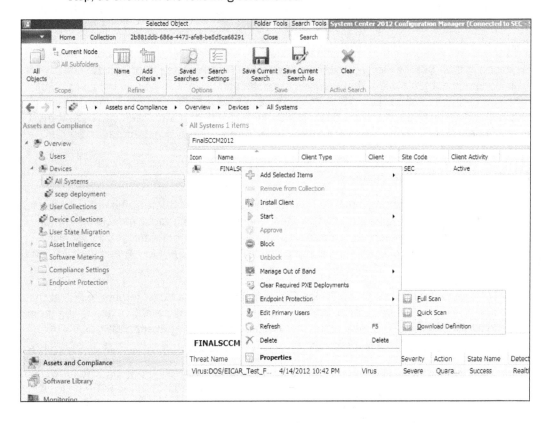

6. It's usually a good idea to wait for about 10 minutes after sending the download definition command before proceeding to the next step. This will allow for the target client to download the new definition file before you kick off a scan.

7. To force a full scan, right-click again on the PC's name, select **Endpoint Protection**, and then left-click on **Full Scan**. Click on **OK** on the information pop-up window to complete the task.

How it works...

As you can see from this recipe, SCEP's integration with the right-click menu in SCCM 2012 makes most operational tasks a snap to complete. Typically, the hardest part of the procedure is finding the target system in a list of potentially thousands of workstations and servers.

This is mitigated by the built-in search function of the SCCM console; by going to the **All Systems** collection and searching there, you are guaranteed to find any machine on your network that has an SCCM client. In a large corporate network with tens of thousands of systems, searching the **All Systems** collection can take a while to return results. If you are certain that the PC you are looking for is a member of smaller sub-collection, it may be less time-consuming to search against the smaller collection.

It's also worth mentioning that the definition source your clients will go to for a new definition is defined in their SCEP policy. For example, if your SCEP policy listed WSUS as the first definition source, then a client that receives the definition update command will go to WSUS for a new definition. Meaning, if WSUS does not have a newer SCEP definition than the client has, nothing will happen. If you are dealing with an outbreak and want clients to have the absolute newest definitions, it is a good idea to perform a manual synchronization of your definition update sources beforehand.

Pushing tasks to multiple systems:

But wait, what if you're getting malware hits from multiple PCs all at the same time and you want all of them to run a full scan with the latest definitions? Well, you're in luck, except for the part where multiple machines on your network are detecting malware; you can select multiple machines in a collection at the same time by using the *Shift* key, then right-click, and push a SCEP task to all of them at the same time.

A word of caution though, it's probably not a good idea to select a huge number of PCs at the same time to do this. Selecting every computer in the **All Systems** collection and telling them all to do a full scan would probably result in a **Resume Generating Event** (**RGE**), as it would likely bring your network to a screeching halt.

If you are dealing with a major virus outbreak and you want every computer on your network to do a full scan for peace of mind, it's probably a better idea to modify existing SCEP policies to perform a full scan in the near future, rather than waiting for normally scheduled scan time to come around. It takes a little while for policy changes to replicate, but the full scans will run, in a smoother staggered fashion.

Using SCEP reports to verify task completion

Being able to launch a SCEP task remotely is great, but any anti-virus administrator worth his or her salt needs to be at least a little bit paranoid. Therefore, this recipe will walk you through the process of using SCEP's reporting capabilities to verify that your commands have been executed successfully. Something as vital to network security as malware event remediation should never be a "fire and forget" scenario.

In this recipe, we will be verifying that definition update command has been completed by using SCCM 2012's reporting function. It is important to remember that although SCCM 2012 is designed to have faster reporting capabilities than previous versions, nothing in SCCM is instant. So, if you have just followed the preceding recipe to force an unscheduled definition update, wait a few minutes before running a report.

Getting ready

In order to complete this recipe, you'll need to utilize an account that has at least the SCEP administrator's SCCM role assigned to it. You will also need access to your SCCM server's reporting capability.

How to do it...

Follow these steps:

1. Log into your SCCM CAS server and launch your SCCM 2012 management console.

2. Navigate to `Monitoring | Overview | Reporting | Reports | Endpoint Protection` and launch the **Computer Malware Details** report, as shown in the following screenshot:

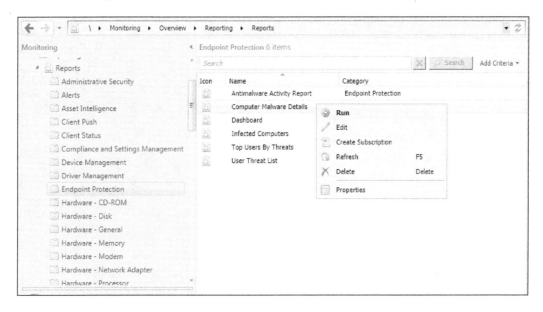

3. The report will open with the bottom three fields empty. In the first field titled **Device Filter**, simply enter a % sign and press *Tab* to move to the next field.

4. The **Collection Name** field should now become available. If you know the collection name from memory, simply type it in. Otherwise, click on the **Values** button and select a collection with your target system as a member from the list.

5. The **Computer Name** field should now be available; you can either type the name of the target machine, or click on the **Values** button and select it from the list.

6. Click on the **View Report** button to run the report.

7. Once the report is complete, locate the **Antimalware Definition Version** field and compare it to the newest definition that is available from your Update Source, as shown in the following screenshot:

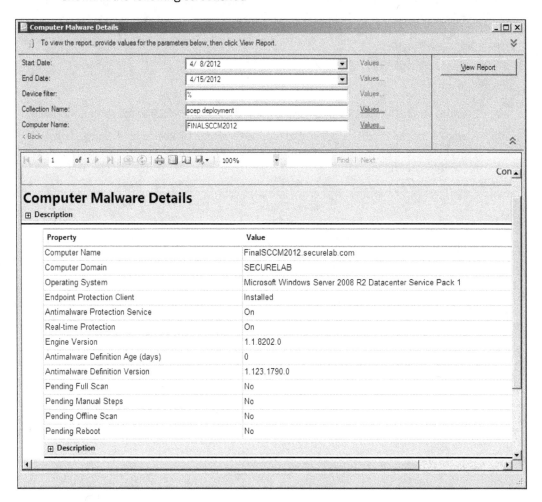

How it works...

Although the name of the **Computer Malware Details** report may be a bit misleading, it is the best place to quickly check the definition status of a single client. It is essentially an amalgamation of the computer details report and the malware details report that were part of SCEPs predecessor, Forefront Endpoint Protection.

The process for confirming the definition version your update source currently possesses varies based on your chosen update source. If you are using SCCM as the primary update source, then I suggest following the first recipe in this chapter, *Checking that your SCCM server has up-to-date SCEP definitions*, to check the version number of the SCEP definition that your SCCM server is currently pushing out.

Utilizing the SCEP dashboard

Dashboards, where would the modern AV administrator be without them? A good dashboard ties large amount of relevant data into a single location and gives the administrator the ability to quickly ascertain his or her environment's overall health at a glance.

SCEP has two dashboards. One is built into the SCCM console itself, the other is accessible through SQL Reporting Services (which means it can be accessed remotely in a web browser).

For this recipe, we will be focusing on the SCCM console-based dashboard as it is the more useful of the two, allowing you to quickly perform tasks based on the information it contains. In this example, we will be ascertaining the definition health status of our clients and taking actions to resolve a deficiency.

Getting ready

For this recipe, you will need to be utilizing an account that has at least the SCEP administrator role assignment attached to it.

How to do it...

Follow these steps:

1. Log into your SCCM CAS server and launch your SCCM 2012 management console.
2. Navigate to `Monitoring | Overview | System Center 2012 Endpoint Protection Status`.

3. Click on the drop-down window under **Collection** and select the collection you wish to evaluate. Note that you will only be presented with a list of collections that have had SCEP deployed to them; if you're in the middle of a pilot for SCEP, this might be very limited subset of collections. When you have gone production-wide with SCEP and deployed to the **All Systems** collection, you will be able to see information on all of your SCEP clients at once. Refer to the following screenshot:

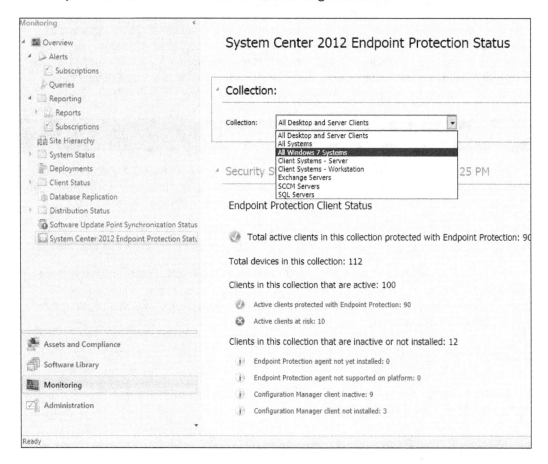

4. Scroll down to the **Operational State** panel. On the right-hand side, you should see a column titled **Definition Status on Computers**, as shown in the following screenshot:

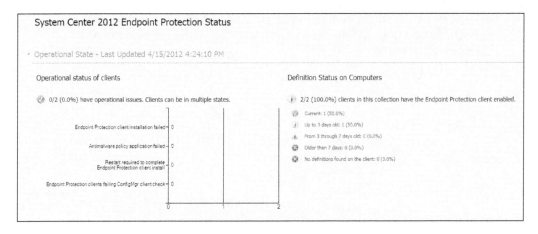

5. Notice the five items under **Definition Status on Computers** in blue. These are actually links that, when clicked on, will create a temporary collection which contains all of the computers that fall into a given category.

6. Click on the link that reads **Up to 3 days old: 1 (50.0%)**.

7. Your view should automatically be moved to the **Assets and Compliance** tab and you will be looking at a collection of PCs that have definitions which are up to three days old. Refer to the following screenshot:

8. Right-click on a computer in this list and select **Endpoint Protection**, **Download Definition** to remediate the definition status on the targeted client, as shown in the following screenshot:

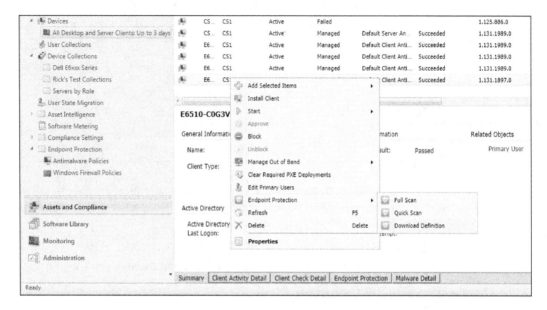

9. To return to the SCEP dashboard, click on the **Monitoring** button in the bottom left-hand side of the console.

10. After waiting for a reasonable amount of time (10 minutes or more), you can force the dashboard to be re-populated with current data by clicking on the **Run Summarization** button at the top of console.

Using MpCmdRun remotely

While using the SCCM console to administer, SCEP is always the preferred method; you may find yourself in a situation where you will need to perform SCEP tasks without the use of the SCCM console. If there was a major virus outbreak on your network and SCCM was knocked offline, it would be critical to maintain control of your SCEP clients.

Additionally, you may have staff members that need to be able to launch full scans and force definition updates remotely, but you do not wish to grant them access to the SCCM console. This recipe will show you how to leverage MpCmdRun.exe and a great free utility from Microsoft named PsExec to accomplish SCEP administration without the SCCM console.

Getting ready

For this recipe, you will need to be using an account that has local administrator privileges on the targeted PC. You will also need to download PsExec from the following website:

```
http://technet.microsoft.com/en-us/sysinternals/bb897553
```

How to do it...

Follow these steps:

1. You'll be running `PsExec.exe` from your own workstation. The exe needs to be run with a command prompt with elevated privileges.

2. If this is your first time running PsExec, you will have to agree to **EULA**.

3. To force a remote PC to run a full scan, execute the following command:

   ```
   psexec \\TargetPCsName "C:\Program Files\Microsoft Security
   Client\Antimalware\mpcmdrun.exe" -scan -2
   ```

4. The value **-scan -2** indicates that a full scan should be run.

5. If the command was successful, then eventually the following syntax will be returned:

   ```
   Scan starting...
   Scan finished.
   C:\Program Files\Microsoft Security Client\Antimalware\mpcmdrun.
   exe exited on TargetPCsName with error code 0.
   ```

    Note that error code 0 in this case indicates success. Also keep in mind that although the message states that the scan is finished, it is likely still running on the target PC.

6. Next, we will send a remote PC a command to retrieve a full definition update directly from the Microsoft Malware Protection Center on the Internet. This command would be useful when attempting to stamp out a spreading infection, as any definition update that comes from MMPC will be the absolute newest available definition file:

   ```
   psexec \\TargetPCsName "C:\Program Files\Microsoft Security
   Client\Antimalware\mpcmdrun.exe" -SignatureUpdate -MMPC
   ```

7. If the command was successful, the following syntax will be returned:

   ```
   Signature update started . . .
   Signature update finished.
   C:\Program Files\Microsoft Security Client\Antimalware\mpcmdrun.
   exe exited on TargetPCsName with error code 0.
   ```

8. Finally, we will be executing an MpCmdRun command that will collect all of the SCEP log files on a target PC into a single directory for easy retrieval. This would be very useful if you're in the process of troubleshooting an outbreak and you've lost access to SCEP reports in SCCM.

   ```
   psexec \\TargetPCsName "C:\Program Files\Microsoft Security
   Client\Antimalware\mpcmdrun.exe" -getfiles
   ```

9. Once the command has completed successfully, you should see the following syntax:

   ```
   Files successfully created in C:\ProgramData\Microsoft\Microsoft
   Antimalware\Support\MpSupportFiles.cab
   ```

10. The preceding file location is located on the target PC; you will need to browse its file system to retrieve the cab file.

How it works...

MpCmdRun.exe is a very useful executable file that can be found on any PC or server that has a SCEP client installed. By using PsExec.exe, we are able to execute remote SCEP commands either in crisis situation or as part of normal administrative procedures.

If an administrator is going to routinely be performing any of the tasks in this recipe, it might make sense to build MpCmdRun into a script.

Additional MpCmdRun functions:

The options in this recipe represent just a handful of the tasks the MpCmdRun can be used for. For your reference, the complete usage output for MpCmdRun can be found as follows:

```
Usage:
MpCmdRun.exe [command] [-options]


Command Description
    -? / -h Displays all available options for this tool
    -Scan [-ScanType #] [-File <path> [-DisableRemediation]] Scans for
malicious software
    -Trace [-Grouping #] [-Level #] Starts diagnostic tracing
    -GetFiles Collects support information
    -RemoveDefinitions [-All] Restores the installed signature definitions
to a previous backup copy or to the original default set of signatures
    [-DynamicSignatures]    Removes only the dynamically downloaded
signatures
    -SignatureUpdate [-UNC [-Path <path>] | -MMPC] Checks for new
definition updates
```

    -Restore -Name <name> [-All] Restore the most recently or all
quarantined item(s) based on threat name

    -AddDynamicSignature [-Path] Loads a dynamic signature

    -ListAllDynamicSignatures List the loaded dynamic signatures

    -RemoveDynamicSignature [-SignatureSetID] Removes a dynamic signature

Additional Information:

Support information will be in the following directory:

c:\ProgramData\Microsoft\Microsoft Antimalware\Support

    -Scan [-ScanType value]

        0 Default, according to your configuration

        1 Quick scan

        2 Full system scan

        3 File and directory custom scan

        [-File <path>] Indicates the file or directory to be scanned,
only valid for custom scan.

        [-DisableRemediation]

            This option is valid only for custom scan.

            When specified:

            - File exclusions are ignored.

            - Archive files are scanned.

            - Actions are not applied after detection.

            - Event log entries are not written after detection.

            - Detections from the custom scan are not displayed in
the user interface.

    Return code is

    0   if no malware is found or malware is successfully remediated
and no additional user action is required

    2   if malware is found and not remediated or additional user
action is required to complete remediation or there is error in scanning.
Please check History for more information.

    -Trace [-Grouping value] [-Level value]

        Begins tracing Microsoft Antimalware Service's actions.

        You can specify the components for which tracing is enabled and

        how much information is recorded.

        If no component is specified, all the components will be logged.

If no level is specified, the Error, Warning and Informational levels will be logged. The data will be stored in the support directory as a file having the current timestamp in its name and bearing the extension BIN.

[-Grouping]

0x1	Service
0x2	Malware Protection Engine
0x4	User Interface
0x8	Real-Time Protection
0x10	Scheduled actions
0x20	NIS/GAPA

[-Level]

0x1	Errors
0x2	Warnings
0x4	Informational messages
0x8	Function calls
0x10	Verbose
0x20	Performance

-GetFiles

Gathers the following log files and packages them together in a compressed file in the support directory

- Any trace files from Microsoft Antimalware Service
- The Windows Update history log
- All Microsoft Antimalware Service events from the System event log
- All relevant Microsoft Antimalware Service registry locations
- The log file of this tool
- The log file of the signature update helper tool

-RemoveDefinitions

Restores the last set of signature definitions

[-All]

Removes any installed signature and engine files. Use this option if you have difficulties trying to update signatures.

[-DynamicSignatures]

Removes all Dynamic Signatures.

-SignatureUpdate

Checks for new definition updates

[-UNC [-Path <path>]]

Performs update directly from UNC file share specified in <path>

If -Path is not specified, update will be performed directly from the preconfigured UNC location

[-MMPC]

Performs update directly from Microsoft Malware Protection Center

-Restore -Name <name>

Restores the most recently quarantined item based on threat name

One Threat can map to more than one file

[-All]

Restores all the quarantined items based on name

-AddDynamicSignature -Path <path>

Adds a Dynamic Signature specified by <path>

-ListAllDynamicSignatures

Lists SignatureSet ID's of all Dynamic Signatures added to the client via SpyNet and MPCMDRUN -AddDynamicSignature

-RemoveDynamicSignature -SignatureSetID <SignatureSetID>

Removes a Dynamic Signature specified by <SignatureSetID>

6
Management Tasks

In this chapter, we will cover:

- ▸ Verifying that SCEP clients are installed on all systems
- ▸ Changing control with SCEP policies
- ▸ Using SCEP policy templates
- ▸ Merging client policies
- ▸ Responding to SCEP alerts

Introduction

This chapter will cover SCEP management tasks, the daily, weekly, and monthly tasks that you want to carry out to ensure that your SCEP environment is staying healthy. To say it another way, this chapter covers care and feeding tasks.

The recipes cover topics such as monitoring for clients on your network that do not have the SCEP client running when they are supposed to, as well as ensuring that you're prepared for disaster if one should ever occur.

Verifying that SCEP clients are installed on all systems

One of the biggest challenges for AV administrators is ensuring that every Windows PC or server on your network has anti-malware solution installed and running. For whatever reason, it's inevitable that someone will stick an unprotected PC on your network. Finding those PCs and remediating the issue quickly is vital.

The built-in SCEP reports will do a good job of maintaining awareness for the collections to which SCEP has been deployed; but unless you've elected to deploy SCEP to the **All Systems** collection, maintaining awareness for your SCCM environment as a whole is another matter. This recipe will first show you how to create a collection with a query that lists all of the PCs that have SCEP installed, and then show you how to build a second collection that shows you the PCs that are not in the first collection. This will tell you which systems do not have SCEP installed; this is sometimes referred to as creating a "does not" collection. As complicated as this might sound, it will make sense by the end.

If you have elected to deploy SCEP to your built-in **All Systems** collection, this recipe might not be necessary for you. Even so, if you're new to SCCM, creating a "does not" collection will be an important skill to have.

Getting ready

In order to complete this recipe, you'll need to utilize an account that has the SCCM full administrator's role assigned to it.

How to do it...

Follow these steps:

1. Log into your SCCM CAS server and launch your SCCM 2012 management console.
2. Navigate to `Assets and Compliance | Overview | Device Collections`.
3. In the upper left-hand side of the interface, click on the **Create Device Collection** button.
4. Give the new collection a descriptive name. It's always a good idea to add some comments that may help you recall at a later date the purpose for which this collection was created (this will also gain you favor with your co-workers).

5. In the **Limiting collection** field, click on the **Browse...** button and select the **All Systems** collection. Click on **Next** to proceed, as shown in the following screenshot:

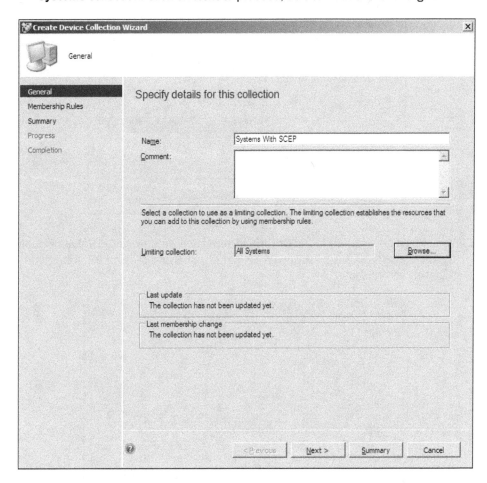

6. On the **Membership Rules** page, click on the **Add Rule** button and select **Query Rule** from the options. The **Query Rules Properties** window should appear.

7. Start by giving the rule a name and then click on **Edit Query Statement**. The **Query Statement Properties** window should appear.

8. Switch to the **Criteria** tab and click on the button labeled with a yellow starburst, the **Criterion Properties** window should appear.

9. Click on the **Select** button under the **Where** field to bring up the **Select Attribute** window. Refer to the following screenshot:

10. Click on the drop-down menu next to **Attribute Class** and select **Add/Remove Programs** from the list.

11. Click on the drop-down menu next to the **Attribute** field and select **Display Name** from the list. Click on **OK** to close the window, as shown in the following screenshot:

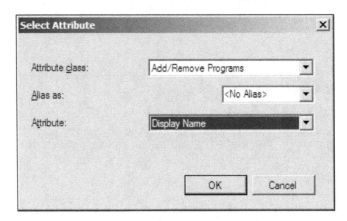

12. You should be returned to the **Criterion Properties** window. In the **Value** field, enter `System Center 2012 Endpoint Protection` and click on **OK**. Refer to the following screenshot:

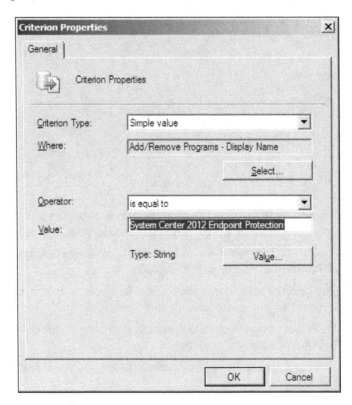

13. You should be returned to the **Query Statement Properties** window, where there should now be an entry in the list of criteria. We now have to repeat the process for 64 bit systems. Click on the button marked with a starburst again.

14. Click on the **Select** button under the **Where** field and the **Select Attribute** window should appear.

15. Click on the drop-down button next to **Attribute class** and select **Add/Remove Programs (64)**. Click on the drop-down button next to the **Attribute** field and select **Display Name**. Click on **OK** to close the window.

16. You should now be looking at the **Criterion Properties** window. In the **Value** field, enter System Center 2012 Endpoint Protection and click on **OK** to close the window. Refer to the following screenshot:

17. This should take you back to the **Query Rule Properties** window. There should now be two entries in the **Criteria** field. SCCM will default to putting an **And** value between them, you must change this to an **Or** value for this procedure to work correctly. To do this, right-click on the word **And**, select **And/Or** from the short cut menu. This should change **And** to an **Or**. Click on **OK** to close the window, as shown in the following screenshot:

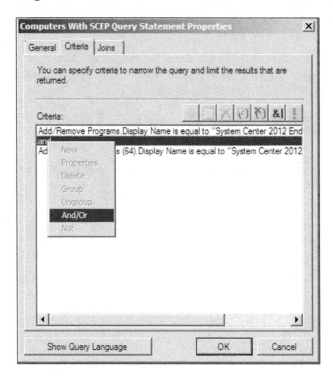

18. At this point, you should be looking at the **Create Device Collection Wizard** again. If all changes are applied correctly, you should now have a single item under **Membership rules**, as shown in the following screenshot:

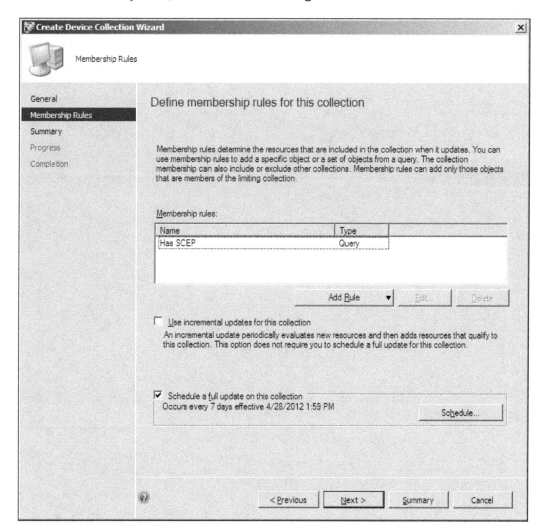

19. Click on **Next** twice to proceed through the **Summary** and **Progress** windows. If all updates were successful, you should be presented with a big green checkmark on the **Completion** screen (you just have to love big green checkmarks!). Refer to the following screenshot:

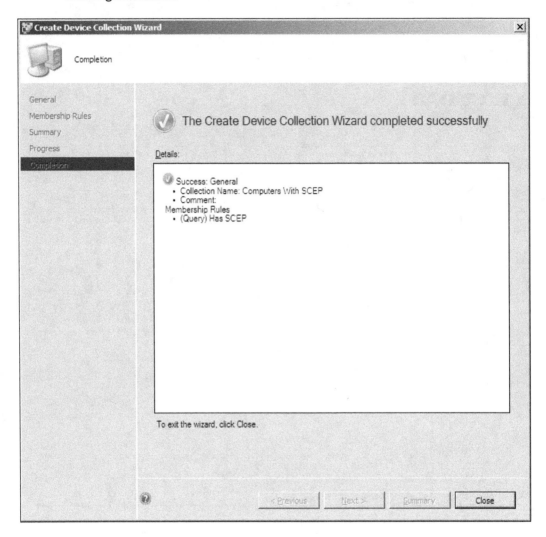

20. Under **Devices** in the **Assets and Compliance** window, you should see the newly created collection. In the first few minutes after you created the collection, it may be empty as it is waiting for the membership rule to process. Eventually, it will be populated with a complete list of all the systems that have SCEP installed.

21. Next, we will be creating a collection to find the systems that do not have SCEP installed. To do this, the first thing we need to know is the **Collection ID** of the collection we just created. To find the **Collection ID**, simply right-click on the **Computers With SCEP** collection. The **Collection ID** can be found at the bottom of the **General** tab. Record this value in a text file. Refer to the following screenshot:

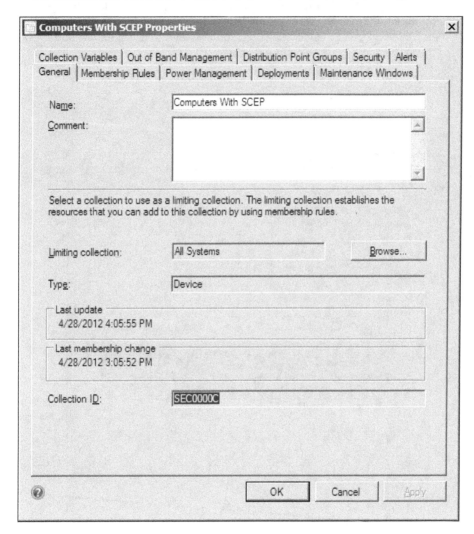

22. Navigate to `Assets and Compliance | Overview | Device Collections` and click on the **Create Device Collection** button.

23. You should again be looking at the **Create Device Collection** wizard. Give the collection a name and add some meaningful comments.

24. Next to the **Limiting Collections** field, click on **Browse** and select the **All Systems Collection**. Click on **Next** to proceed.

25. Click **Add Rule** and select **Query Rule**. The **Query Rule Properties** window should pop up. Give the new rule a name, and then click **Edit Query Statement**.

26. The **Query Statement Properties** window should appear. Click on the **Show Query Language** button. In the **Query Statement** field, first remove the existing text and then paste or type in the following text. You will need to change the value **XXXXXXXX** to the Collection ID which you found in step 21.

```
SELECT SMS_R_System.ResourceID, SMS_R_System.ResourceType,
SMS_R_System.Name, SMS_R_System.SMSUniqueIdentifier, SMS_R_System.
ResourceDomainORWorkgroup, SMS_R_System.Client
FROM SMS_R_System
WHERE Client = 1
AND ClientType = 1
AND ResourceId NOT IN (SELECT ResourceID FROM SMS_CM_RES_COLL_
XXXXXXXX)
```

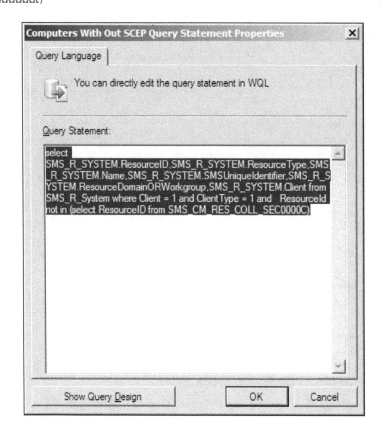

27. Click on **OK** and continue to do so until you are returned to the **Create Device Collection Wizard**.

28. Click on **Next** on the **Summary** and **Progress** pages and **Close** on the **Completion** page.

29. You will again need to wait a few minutes for the collection membership to process.

30. Once the member of the **Does Not Have SCEP Collection** has been updated, you can spot-check your work by right-clicking on any members of the collection and left-clicking on **Start/Resource Explorer**. Then, expand the **Hardware** object and select **Add/Remove Programs** or **Add Remove Programs (64)**, depending on the OS. System Center 2012 Endpoint Protection should not appear in the list. Refer to the following screenshot:

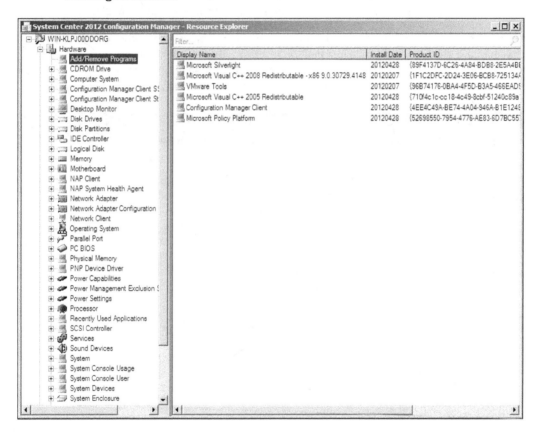

How it works...

If this was your first foray into WQL and query-based collections, then congratulations, the headache you are feeling right now will subside. Just remember, the more time you spend playing with collection queries, the more you will discover its almost unlimited usefulness.

One important thing to remember, when you are trying to remediate missing SCEP clients, is that because we've tied the membership of the "does not have" SCEP collection to the "does have" SCEP collection; you will first need to manually update the collection membership of the "does have" SCEP collection to see any change in the "does not have" SCEP collection. For this reason it might be a good idea to make the "does not have" collection a sub-collection of the "does have" collection. That way when you right-click on the first collection, you can simply check the box in the dialog message to have it also update all sub-collections at the same time.

In addition, it's worth noting that Hardware Inventory is the basis for whether or not SCCM thinks that a given application is installed on a system. By default, Hardware Inventory only runs once a week, so the information that SCCM has on installed applications could be dated. It is possible to adjust the frequency of hardware inventories in client settings.

Changing control with SCEP policies

With anything that could have as much impact on a client machine as anti-virus policy can, it's important to have some degree of change control. Whatever workflow or procedures your organization uses for changing control should be applied to the modification and deployment of SCEP policies. This recipe will focus on showing you how to verify that change control procedures are being utilized with the management of SCEP policies.

After completing this recipe, you will know how to check who created a policy, who the last person to modify the policy was, and where the policy has been deployed. Not to mention, verifying who has rights to modify and deploy the policy.

Getting ready

To complete this recipe, you will need to be using an account that has at least the SCEP administrator role granted to it.

How to do it...

Follow these steps:

1. Log into your SCCM CAS server and launch the SCCM 2012 management console.
2. Navigate to `Assets and Compliance` | `Overview` | `Endpoint Protection` | `Antimalware Policies`.

3. Select a policy from the **Antimalware Policies** list and locate the **File Properties** section at the bottom of the User Interface. Refer to the following screenshot:

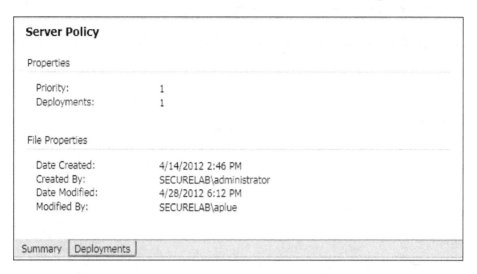

4. Under **File Properties**, you'll be able to determine when the policy was created and who created it, as well as the last user to modify the policy in any way.

5. To see the collections to which this policy has been deployed, switch to the **Deployments** tab, as shown in the following screenshot:

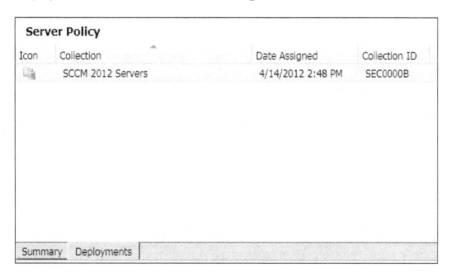

6. To remove the policy from a collection to which it has been assigned, simply right-click on it in the **Deployments** tab and select **Delete**.

7. To view which users or groups have rights to modify a policy, right-click on it in the **Antimalware Policies** list and select **Properties**. Select **Security** from the column on the left-hand side, as shown in the following screenshot:

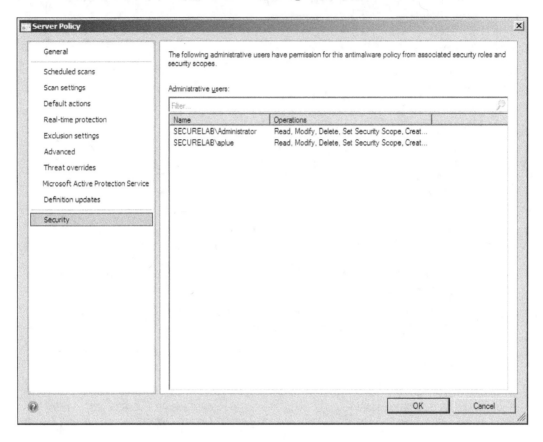

8. If you wish to change who has rights to modify policies, you will need to update the security roles they have been assigned in the **Administration** panel of the SCCM console.

How it works...

SCCM 2012 maintains awareness of whom and when SCEP polices are being modified. This information is reflected in the SCCM console for easy reference. Having this information on hand will allow you to enforce change control for SCEP polices.

Using SCEP policy templates

One the best features in FEP was the use of policy templates. Microsoft included a list of pre-configured policies for just about every type of server-based application that they offer (SQL, Exchange, IIS, and so on). These policy templates were based off Microsoft's best practices for OS-level anti-virus products and included all the exclusions and exceptions needed to maximize performance, while maintaining a proper level of security.

Luckily, Microsoft has decided to include these policy templates in SCEP, but the way they are accessed and utilized is a little bit different from before. In this recipe, we will be building a policy for an Exchange 2010 server.

Getting ready

For this recipe, you will need to be utilizing an account that has at least the SCEP administrator role assignment attached to it.

How to do it...

Follow these steps:

1. Log into your SCCM CAS server and launch your SCCM 2012 management console, and navigate to Assets and Compliance | Overview | Endpoint Protection | Antimalware Policies.

2. Click on the **Import** button on the top left-hand side of the user interface; an explorer window should open up to display a long list of XML files, as shown in the following screenshot:

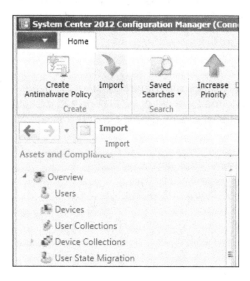

3. Locate the file titled **FEP_Default_Exchange** and select it, then click on the **Open** button.

4. The **Create Antimalware Policy** wizard should open with its options pre-populated, as shown in the following screenshot:

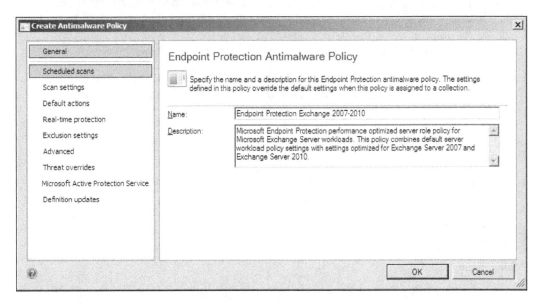

5. You have the option to change any settings that are not in line with your organization's policies. Once you are happy with the policy, click on **OK** to close the wizard.

6. Deploy the policy to a collection that contains the intended target PCs. In this example, you would want to choose a collection that contains only Exchange servers. Such a collection would need to be created with a query that identifies Exchange servers by looking for Exchange 2010 in their **Add/Remove** programs.

How it works...

The SCEP product team has worked with different server application product teams to build policy templates that include the ideal set of exclusions and exceptions. Although the XML files for these policy templates start with the letters FEP, they are still valid for use in SCEP.

Merging policy templates:

One way in which policy templates could be useful is to merge them with your existing general server policy. In this scenario, your own server policy would be chosen as the base during the merge. The end result would be a policy that has all your standard settings for scheduled scan times, update sources, and so on, and the additional settings for the necessary folder and file exclusions that Microsoft recommends to keep the given application running at peak performance.

If you have a server that runs two or more Microsoft applications, you could also merge the policies for both applications to create a new super policy that includes the exclusions for both products.

Merging client policies

Policy merging is a new feature in SCEP that allows you to combine two or more SCEP policies into one new policy. This is useful for consolidating polices, and for keeping your list of available policies to a more manageable size.

Getting ready

In order to complete this recipe, you'll need to utilize an account that has at least the Endpoint Protection Managers role assigned to it.

How to do it...

Follow these steps:

1. Log into your SCCM CAS server and launch your SCCM 2012 management console.
2. Navigate to `Assets and Compliance` | `Overview` | `Endpoint Protection` | `Antimalware Policies`.
3. From the **Antimalware Policies** list, select the first policy of the group that you're planning to merge and hold down the control key on your keyboard.
4. Select the second policy you are planning to merge and click on the **Merge** button at the top of the user interface.
5. The **Merge Policies** window should appear and verify that all the policies you wish to merge are included in the list.

6. Enter a name in the **New Policy Name** field. In the **Base Policy** field, select the policy that you believe most closely resembles what you envision the final product to look like. Click on **OK** to proceed, as shown in the following screenshot:

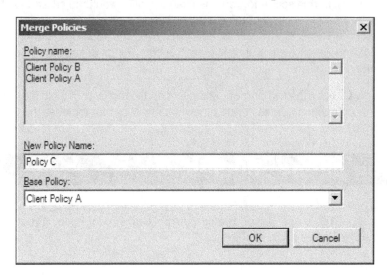

7. The new merged policy should now appear in **Antimalware Policies** list.

The logic that drives what settings will make it into the newly created merged policy is fairly simple. All the settings that are in the policy you've selected as the base will make it into the new policy. If there are any conflicts between the two policies, the settings in the policy that was selected as the base policy will win. Any settings that are in the secondary policy and not in the base policy will be added to the new merged policy.

Responding to SCEP alerts

So it's 2 A.M. on a Tuesday, you're the SCEP administrator on call, and you've just been woken up for an alert for a malware outbreak. What do you do? This recipe will show you where to go in the SCCM console to review the alert, as well as provide some guidance on what actions to take.

For the example outlined in this recipe, we will be responding to a situation where malware has been detected on a few PCs in the **All Systems** collection, which has an alert for malware detection assigned to it, and the number of PCs with the malware in question was great enough to trigger the malware outbreak alert as well.

Getting ready

For this recipe, you will need to utilize an account that has at least the SCEP administrator role assignment attached to it.

How to do it...

Follow these steps:

1. Log into your SCCM CAS server and launch your SCCM 2012 management console.

2. Navigate to `Monitoring | Overview | Alerts`.

3. Any alerts that have been recently triggered will be marked with the red **X** icon and have an alert state of **Active**.

4. Locate and select the alert labeled **Malware detection for collection: All Systems**. At the bottom of the UI, click on the **Machines** tab to see list of PCs that generated this alert, as shown in the following screenshot:

5. Pay special attention to the columns labeled **Action Success** and **Pending Action**. This information will inform you of whether or not SCEP was successful in zapping the malware or if there are any additional steps, such as reboot, left outstanding for the malware to be fully removed.

6. Next, find the alert labeled **Malware outbreak alert for a collection: All Systems** and click on the **Malware** tab to see a list of the malware threats that have been detected on multiple computers, as shown in the following screenshot:

7. It's a best practice to search for this malware by name against the Microsoft Malware Encyclopedia: `http://www.microsoft.com/security/portal/`. Look for the **Antimalware protection details** section at the bottom of the page. Here, you will find the first version of the SCEP definition file that protects against this threat. This is vitally important. If this is a very recently discovered piece of malware and some SCEP clients are behind in their definitions, then you may be in a situation where either there are more infected clients on your network than you know because it's going undetected, or clients with old definitions may soon contract this malware. In either case, your goal should be to get all your PCs up-to-date with a definition that covers this malware as fast as possible. Refer to the following screenshot:

8. The actions you can take on the **Alerts** page are somewhat limited. You can add comments to an alert, which could be used to inform other SCEP administrators that you are looking into the situation. You can also postpone the alert; this could be useful if you're fighting off an outbreak and simply wish to stop the deluge of e-mail alerts. It's important to note, that postponing an alert will still allow the malware event to be added to your reporting data, it simply stops an e-mail subscription rule from executing.

How it works...

SCEP alerts are a vital tool for SCEP administrators to respond quickly to malware events. In SCCM 2012, Microsoft created something called the High Speed Data Channel to facilitate a five minute or less SLA for malware detections. This means that within five minutes or less after a piece of malware is first detected by a SCEP client, the event data for this detection is available within the SCCM console. If the computer in question is a member of a collection that has a SCEP alert assigned to it and an alert subscription has been created, an e-mail will be generated and delivered to your inbox.

As a best practice, it makes sense to have malware alerts assigned to the **All Systems** collection, as you probably want to know about malware that is detected anywhere on your network. However, if you work for a very large organization with global operations, you may want to break your alerts up into regions. This can be done by assigning alerts to specific collections made up of a given region's PCs, rather than **All Systems**. Either approach is valid, but it's not recommended to do both as this will create redundant alerts for the same event, which can be very confusing at 2 A.M.

7
Reporting

In this chapter, we will cover:

- ▸ Utilizing the system-based SCEP reports
- ▸ Utilizing the user-based SCEP reports
- ▸ Providing access to reports
- ▸ Building custom reports

Introduction

Reporting is the key to keeping your network virus-free. Some readers may object to this statement. Some may believe, it's your client policies or your definition update methodology that are the most important factor in keeping malware off your network. And while these things are important, reporting is the most vital.

It goes without saying that reporting gives you awareness into the status of your client policies and also your current definition status, but that's not why it's so important. Reporting is key, because it enables you to identify trends and common attacking vectors by allowing you to view your environment as a whole over a span of time. This in turn empowers you, the AV admin, to be proactive. It gives you the knowledge you need to plug the dike, to stamp out fires, and deal with small problems before they become massive ones.

The recipes in this chapter will show you how to best leverage the built-in reports for SCEP within SCCM 2012, as well as showing you how to tap into the most unlimited options for custom reporting with Microsoft SQL Report Builder 3.0.

Using the system-based SCEP reports

The six built-in SCEP reports can be broken up into two categories: user-centric reports and system-centric reports. This recipe focuses on the group of system-based reports.We will be executing and interrupting the computer malware details, anti-malware activity report, and infected computers. Although these reports can be accessed either through the SCCM console or with a web browser, for this recipe, we will access them from the SCCM console.

Getting ready

In order to complete this recipe, you'll need to utilize an account that has at least the Endpoint Protection Manager roles assigned to it. If your installation of SCEP is in a lab, or is very new and has not yet detected any malware on your systems, then it's recommended that you utilize Eicar test file to simulate a malware detection. Eicar test file is a completely safe file that all major anti-malware vendors add to their definitions for testing purposes. It can be downloaded from `http://www.eicar.org/`. Please remember to allow up to five minutes, after the time you trigger the Eicar detection, to start executing reports.

How to do it...

Follow these steps:

1. Log into your SCCM CAS server and launch your SCCM 2012 management console.
2. Navigate to `Monitoring\Overview\Reporting\Reports\Endpoint Protection` and select the **Antimalware Activity Report**.
3. Click on **Values** at the end of the **Collection Name** field and select any of the collections to which SCEP has been applied, as shown in the following screenshot:

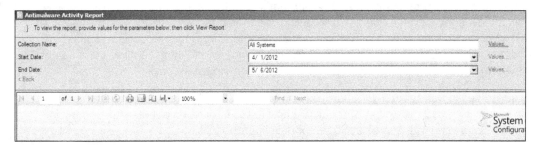

4. Choose **Start Date** and **End Date** and click on **View Report**.

5. Take note of blue links, any of these can be clicked to drill-down and learn more about a given aspect of the report. For now, click on the number value below **Total Remediations**. This should take you to a sub-report titled **Infected Computers**. Refer to the following screenshot:

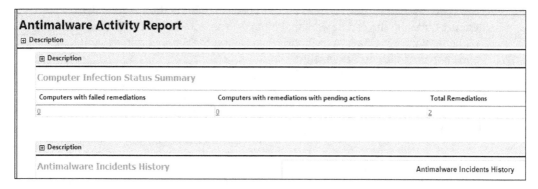

6. Find the PC on which you ran the Eicar test string and click on the name; this will launch the **Computer Malware** details report for this PC, as shown in the following screenshot:

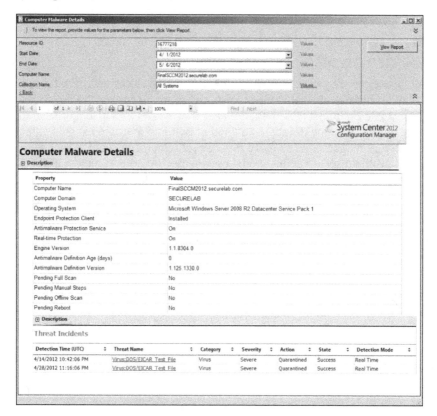

7. To learn more about the malware with which this system has been afflicted, click on the link under **Threat Name**.This will take you to the malware details report. Here, you can see the link that will launch an Internet Explorer browser and direct you to the page within the Microsoft Virus Encyclopedia for this threat.

8. Next, we will export this report in order to distribute it to other users. Click on the **Export** button in the report workspace bar and select **PDF** as the file format. Enter a destination in the **Save As** window and click on the **Save** button to complete, as shown in the following screenshot:

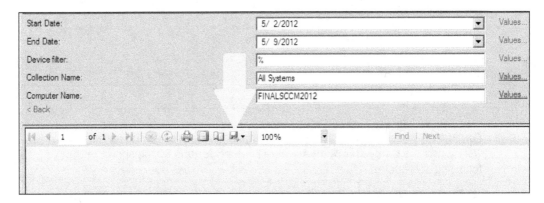

How it works...

One of the biggest improvements in SCEP over FEP is the consolidation of databases. FEP stored data in two different DBs that were separated from the core SCCM DB and SCEP, whereas, SCCM 2012 shares the same database. This means you no longer have to wait for data to be moved from one database to another before a malware event is reflected in your reports. In FEP, it could take up to 45 minutes for a malware event to be reflected in a report. With SCEP, the malware event should be reflected in a report almost instantly once the message is received by the SCCM server (usually within five minutes).

The system-centric group of SCEP reports allows you to quickly look at incidents on multiple PCs, or drill-down to the **Computer Malware Details** report to review the status of a single PC. The **Computer Malware Details** report shows all relevant SCEP client details, such as engine and definition versions, in addition to a history of malware events.

Exporting the **Computer Malware Details** as a PDF will allow you to quickly share information with other users even if they do not have access to the SCCM console or the SQL Reporting Services for your SCCM server.

Utilizing the user-based SCEP reports

The second group of reports in SCEP focuses entirely on the users, which falls in line with Microsoft's mantra of focusing on users within SCCM 2012 as a whole. While the overall user focus provides for things, such as customized application delivery in the rest of SCCM, focus on users in SCEP allows you to monitor your problem children.

Every organization has them; the user that will happily open any attachment and fears no website on the Internet. The good news is that SCEP empowers you to monitor for repeat offenders, regardless what system they may be using.

Getting ready

To complete this recipe, you will need to be using an account that has at least the SCEP administrator role granted to it. You will also need to ensure that you've enabled Active Directory Users discovery in SCCM and that it has completed the discovery at least once before following this recipe.

How to do it...

Follow these steps:

1. Log into your SCCM CAS server and launch your SCCM 2012 management console.

2. Navigate to `\Monitoring\Overview\Reporting\Reports\Endpoint Protection` and right-click on **Top Users By Threats**, and click on **Run**.

3. Select a collection to run this report again by clicking on the **Values** button and choosing a collection. You can also adjust the time span if you wish to do so. Click on the **View Report** button to execute the report.

4. The report will return a list of users ranked by the number of malware events associated with that account, as shown in the following screenshot:

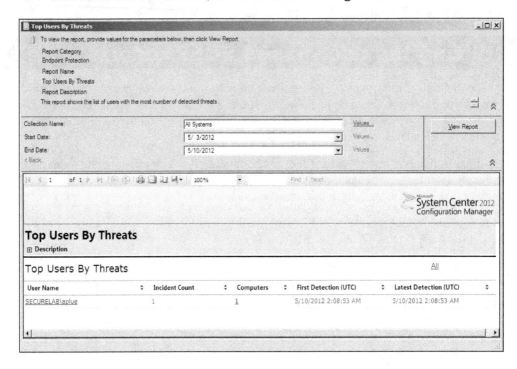

5. To review the particular events a given user has experienced, click on a user name from the list. This will bring up the **User Threat List** report for that account, as shown in the following screenshot:

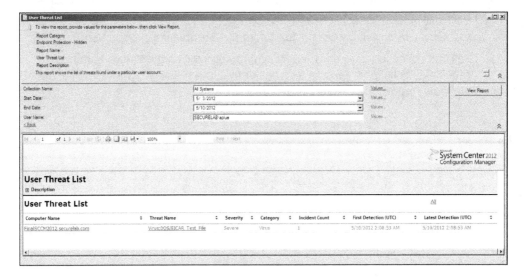

How it works...

As SCEP collects a rich dataset for any malware event that has been detected, it is aware of any user who was logged in at that time. Possessing this information will allow you to identify patterns of behavior that expose your network to risk. That said, it is possible for many types of malware (such as a worm) to show up in a malware report for a computer that a given user was logged into, without the user having done anything.

Providing access to reports

A malware report is only useful if the people with the power to address an issue can access the report. One of the paradigms of integrating your anti-virus with SCCM is the fact that many more people in an organization will now need access to SCCM. While the new role-based privileges alleviate this pain point somewhat, there will likely be some individuals with whom you just are not comfortable giving access to the SCCM console,who will need to access SCEP reporting data.

Luckily, this can be addressed by granting them access to the SCEP reports within SQL Reporting Services. This recipe will walk you through the procedure for doing so.

Getting ready

For this recipe, you will need to utilize an account that has administrator privileges for the SQL Reporting Services instance that is hosting your SCCM reports. This recipe is written from the perspective of being logged into the server that is hosting the reports and running IE locally. The procedure can also be done remotely; just replace **localhost** with the DNS name of the server.

In order to be able to deliver report subscriptions over email, it is required that the SMTP information has been entered into the SQL Reporting Services Configuration Utility and that the corresponding Exchange server allows for the SQL reporting services server to send SMTP traffic through its SMTP connector.

How to do it...

Follow these steps:

1. Log into SQL Reporting Services server and launch Internet Explorer.

2. Browse to the following URL: `http://localhost/Reports/Pages/Folder.aspx`.

3. Proceed to drill down to the directory that hosts your SCEP reports by clicking on `ConfigMgr_XXX` (XXX representing your site code) and then selecting the `Endpoint Protection` directory.

4. To grant user or group of users access to the reports in the directory, click on the **Folder Settings** button and then select **Security** from the left hand-side of the page.

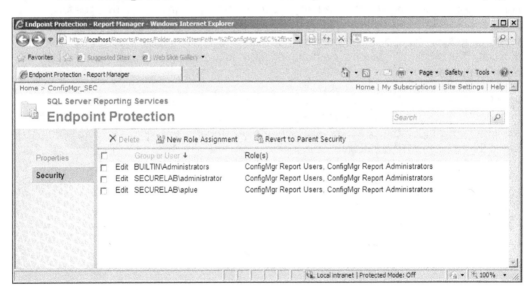

5. Next, click on the **New Role Assignment** button, enter a user or group name in the field provided, and check the boxes for the permissions you wish to grant. At minimum, select the **Browser** and **ConfigMgr Reports Users** roles. Click on **OK** to complete the process.

6. Next, we will create a subscription for the **Dashboard** report, which will deliver it on a scheduled basis over e-mail. Use your browser's back button to return to the root of the Endpoint Protection reports directory.

7. Hover your cursor over the link for the **Dashboard** report for a moment and a gold down arrow icon will appear. Click this and select **Subscribe** from the drop-down menu.

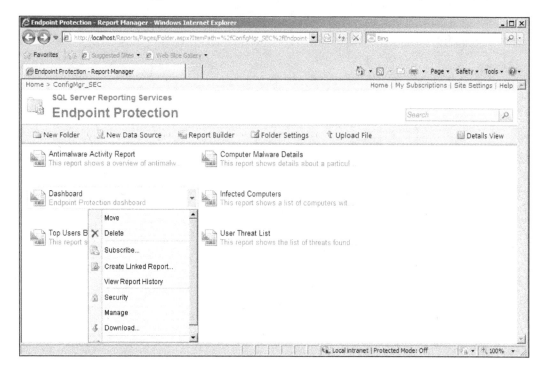

8. Make sure **E-mail** is selected from the drop-down menu at the top of page. You will need to enter a value for the **To:** field and supply a reply address (it does not need to be an actual email account).

9. Select a render format for the e-mail subscription. The PDF format is typically ideal as it can be easily read on both PCs and mobile devices. Refer to the following screenshot:

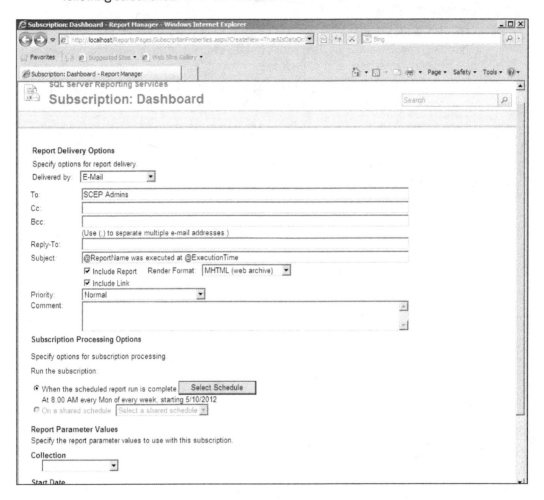

10. Next, set a schedule for the report by clicking on the **Select Schedule** button.

11. Finally, select a collection for this report to be run against and click on **OK** to create the subscription.

How it works...

SQL Reporting Services provides an ideal platform for SCEP reports, because it allows you easily assign access to an Active Directory user or a group and can be relied upon to deliver reports on a schedule. Keeping your admins from setting up an Outlook rule to automatically place the e-mails in the recycling bin is another matter entirely.

Building custom reports

Out of the box, SCCM 2012 contains four hundred and twenty-three pre-built reports. Unfortunately, only six of them pertain to Endpoint Protection. The good news is that with SCCM 2012 comes the release of SQL Report Builder 3.0, which makes it easier than ever for almost anybody to quickly create a customized report based on any of the Endpoint Protection data that SCCM collects and stores in its database. And believe me, you'll be amazed when you peek under the hood and see the wealth of data just waiting there for you to groom and shape as you see it.

For this recipe,we will keep it simple and build a report that shows the count of PCs that have the **Network Inspection Service(NIS)** enabled as well as a count of those that do not have the service enabled. NIS usage is a valuable piece of security data that is not reflected in any of the built-in reports.

Getting ready

For this recipe, you will need to utilize an account that has administrator privileges for the SQL Reporting Services instance that hosts your SCCM reports.

If you have not used Custom Report Builder 3.0 on this server yet, you may need to modify a registry key on the CAS server to ensure it opens the Version 3.0 and not the Version 2.0 of Report Builder. This procedure is outlined at the end of this section.

How to do it...

Follow these steps:

1. Log in to you CAS server and open the SCCM management console.
2. Navigate to `Monitoring\Overview\Reporting\Reports`. In the ribbon on the left-hand side, right-click on **reports** and select **Create Report**.

3. The **Create Report Wizard** window should pop up. In the **Type** section, choose **SQL-based Report**. In the **information** section, enter a name for the report and a description if wish to do so. Next, click on the **Browse** button and choose **Endpoint Protection** and the desired path for this report. Click on the **Next** button to proceed.

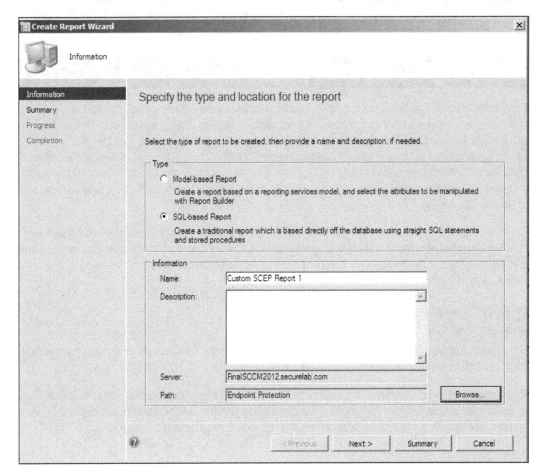

4. On the **Summary** page, review the options you've selected, if everything checks out, click on **Next** to proceed.

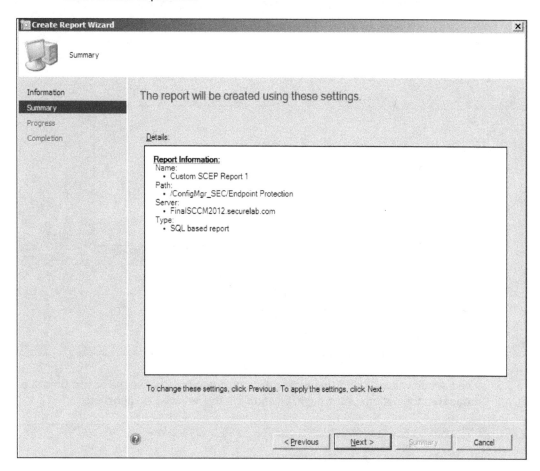

5. Once you click on **Next** on the completion page, the custom report window will disappear and a few moments later, Microsoft SQL Report Builder 3.0 will open. The report we just created in the **Create Report Wizard** should display automatically.

6. To begin, click on the object titled **Table or Matrix** in the center of the window.

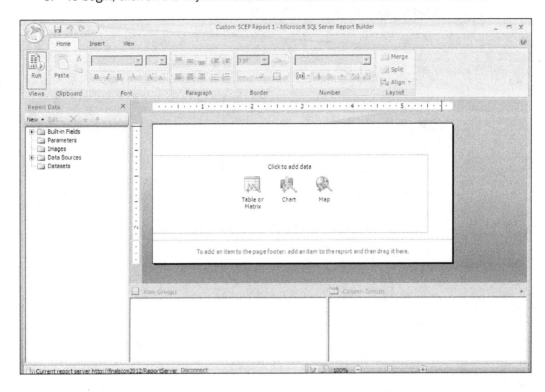

7. A new window titled **New Table or Matrix** should pop up. Choose the option **Create a dataset** at the bottom of the page, as shown in the following screenshot:

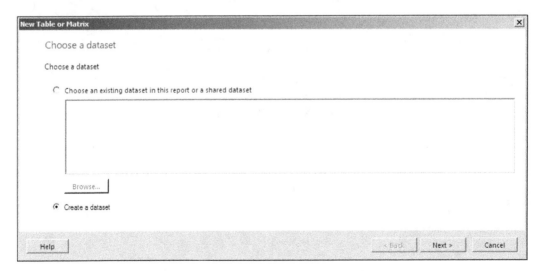

8. On the next page, you'll be choosing a connection to a data source, typically the connection to your SCCM database will already be present and selected. If it's not there, you may have to browse for it. Once you are ready, click on **Next** to proceed.

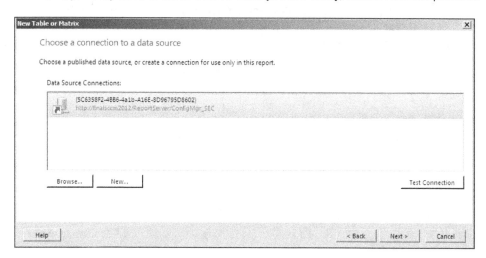

9. You will now be prompted for user credentials, which are needed to access the SCCM database. You have the option of using the credentials with which you are currently logged in with or entering another set of user credentials. Click on **Next** to proceed.

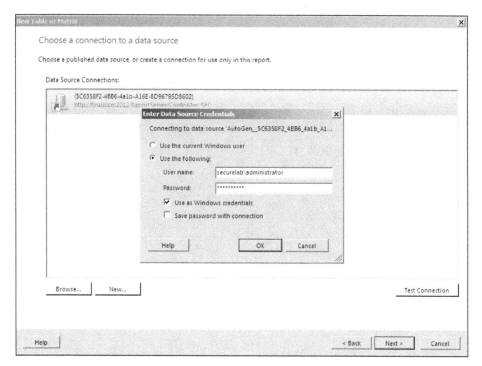

10. Next, select the database view that your report will be tapping into to extract the information about your client's NIS status. To do this, locate **v_GS_ AntimalwareHealthStatus** within the column titled **Database view** and expand it. Scroll down and locate the **NISEnabled** object and check the box next to it. **NISEnabled** should now appear in the **Selectedfields** window. Click on **Next** to move on. Refer to the following screenshot:

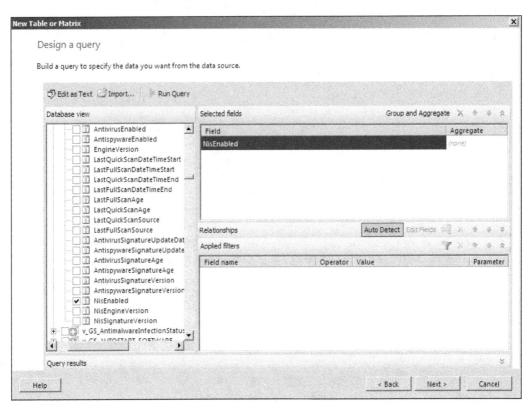

11. On the **Arrange fields** page of the wizard, you will need to drag the **NISEnabled** object to both the **Row Groups** and **Values** window. Once you have **NISEnabled** in the **Values** window, right-click on it and select **Count** from the list. Click on **Next** to proceed.

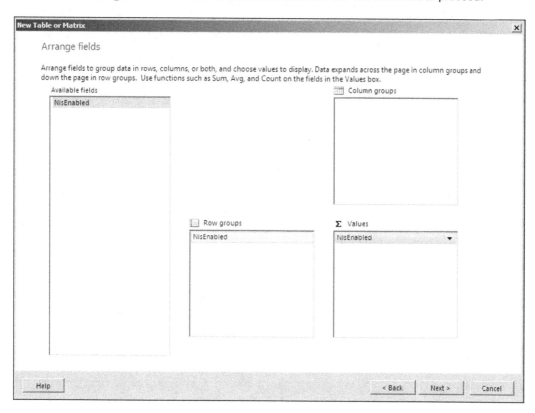

12. On the **Choose the layout** page, select **Show subtotals and grand totals**. You'll also need to enable the option for **Stepped, subtotal above**. Lastly, make sure that you've enabled the option **Expand/collapse groups**. Click on **Next** to proceed. Refer to the following screenshot:

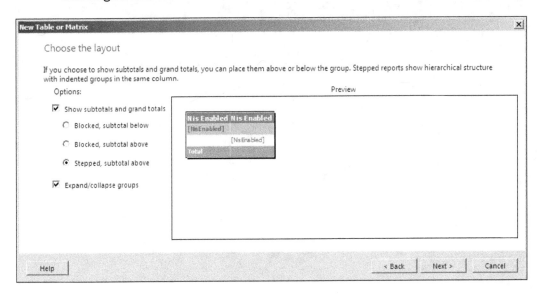

13. On the **Choose a Style** page, you can select a color palate to match your personality or mood. I prefer the calm, relaxing vibe of "ocean". Once you've chosen a style, click on **Finish** and you'll be returned to Report Builder.

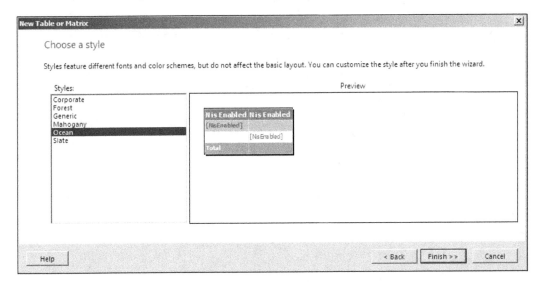

14. Once you are back in Report Builder, you'll have an opportunity to tweak the look of the report. When you are happy with the layout, click on the **Run** button in the upper left-hand corner to test the report out for the first time. Refer to the following screenshot:

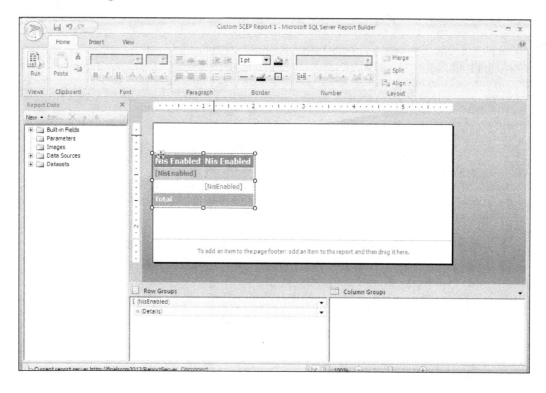

15. If everything works correctly, you'll be presented with a report that lists the total counts of your clients that are running NIS and a count of those that have NIS disabled.

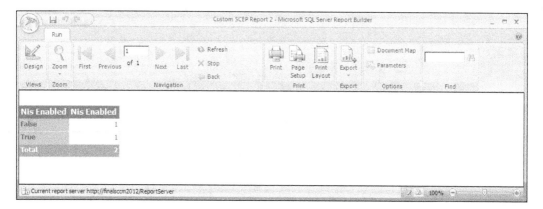

16. Close out of the report preview, save your work in Report Builder and exit out of it as well. You can now run the report whenever you need to do so by browsing to `Monitoring\Overview\Reporting\Reports\Endpoint Protection`.

How it works...

Although the report we've built in this recipe is rather on the simple side, I hope it's allowed you to get your feet wet with custom reporting. Once you understand the basic mechanics of Report Builder and how to tap into SQL views, there's really no limit to the ways you can piece information together and build something that makes your job a little easier.

Setting up SQL Report Builder 3.0 as your default:

Although SQL Report Builder 3.0 comes bundled with SCCM 2012, it is not the default Report Builder on your CAS server until you make a small change to the registry. Until you make this change, your server will automatically try to open in the previous version that was installed on your server when you installed SQL 2008. To make this change, log in as local administrator and complete the following steps:

1. Click on **Start | Run**, type `Regedit`, and hit enter. The registry editor should open.

2. Navigate to: `HKEY_LOCAL_MACHINE\SOFTWARE\Wow6432Node\Microsoft\ConfigMgr10\AdminUI\Reporting`.

3. Open the **ReportBuilderApplicationManifestName** key and change the string to `ReportBuilder_3_0_0_0.application`. Click on **OK** to close **Regedit**.

8
Troubleshooting

In this chapter, we will cover:

- ▶ Resolving client-side definition update issues
- ▶ Fixing SCCM client health issues
- ▶ Resolving false positives
- ▶ Dealing with infections that SCEP cannot resolve

Introduction

Microsoft has put a lot of effort into making the SCCM client for 2012 much more robust than previous versions, and with Windows 7, WMI corruption issues are mostly a thing of the past. But when you've got thousands and thousands of clients deployed, you can bet that at least a few of them experience issues from time to time.

This chapter contains recipes that will guide you through some basic procedures for resolving definition update issues, fixing broken SCCM clients, and getting rid of false positive malware detections.

Resolving client-side definition update issues

If your SCEP clients fall out of date, the approach you will need to take in your troubleshooting efforts will depend largely on which of the five available update mechanisms you selected during the policy creation process. For this recipe, we will be working on a client that has been enabled by the policy to use the SCCM definition packages, WSUS, Microsoft updates, and the Microsoft Malware Protection Center as definition update sources. Leveraging multiple definition update sources is a common scenario that any organization should consider implementing, as it provides redundancy.

Getting ready

In order to complete this recipe, you'll need to utilize an account that has local administrator privileges on the affected client. This recipe will walk you through the process of examining a client which has not been updated for several days. We will examine the logs for a root cause and then remediate any issues we find.

How to do it...

Follow these steps:

1. Log in to the workstation you are troubleshooting and open the SCEP client UI from the system tray.

2. Click on the **Update** tab, take note of the **Definitions created on** and **Definitions last checked** dates. If, like in the following screenshot, the **Definitions last checked** date is significantly closer to the present date and time than the **Definitions created on** date, this would indicate a problem with the update sources this client is trying to utilize.

   This means the client is able to communicate with the update repository on your network, but the update repository does not have a newer definition than the one the client already has. Resolving this issue permanently will likely require some remediation effort on the server and not the client. For now, we will continue to troubleshoot and find out what update sources this client has been attempting to utilize and determine why the client was not able to get out to Microsoft Updates on the web, if the internal update server was severely out of date. Refer to the following screenshot:

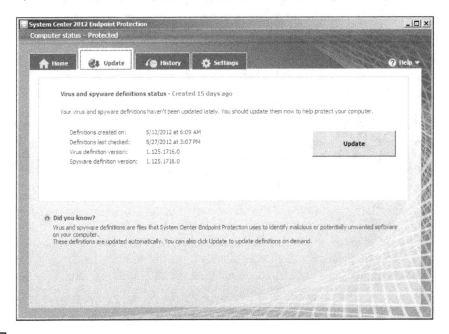

3. Next, we will verify that the client PC has been opted into Microsoft Updates in order to receive definition updates directly from Microsoft. Generally, this should have occurred as a post-image installation task, or through the deployment of a regkey. The fastest way to determine whether opt-in has occurred is to launch Windows Update and look for a message that reads **Get Updates for other Microsoft products**. Refer to the following screenshot:

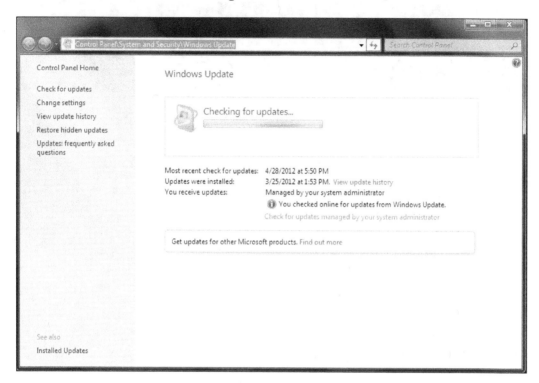

4. If you do not see this message in the Windows Update UI, then your client has already been opted in; the reason it has not pulled definitions from Microsoft Updates is likely network related. This means Microsoft Updates is most likely blocked at the web proxy level. If you do see the message that the client needs to be opted in, click on the blue link titled **Find out more** and agree to the EULA. Refer to the following screenshot:

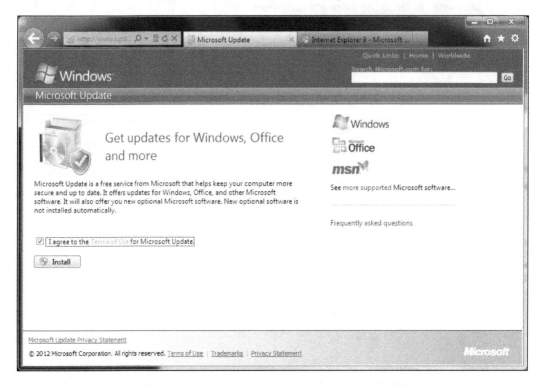

5. If you have just opted in the workstation for Microsoft Updates, return to the SCEP client UI and force an update. While this will resolve the issue temporarily, you should continue to troubleshoot in order to determine why your internal update resources failed.

6. Next, we will review the client's MPLog. To find this log, navigate to `C:\ProgramData\Microsoft\Microsoft Antimalware\Support`. (Note that `Program Data` is normally a hidden folder in Windows.) Open the log in Notepad and place your cursor at the very top of the log. Press *Ctrl* and *F* keys simultaneoulsy to bring up the **Find** window. Type in the word, `updated`, and click on the **Find next** button. This should take you immediately to a log entry similar to the one shown in the following screenshot. The words **updated via MMPC** indicate that this workstation was not able to get an update from any internal resource or to reach Microsoft Updates; it then reached out to the **Microsoft Malware Protection Center** (**MMPC**) to get a definition. As MMPC was the last update source in our policy, we can assume that all other update sources have failed. Refer to the following screenshot:

```
MPLog-04152012-112408 - Notepad                                    _|□|×|
File  Edit  Format  View  Help
  ProcBitmap:0                                                          ▲
  NumInstance:2
  TotalStreamCon:968
  TotalBitmap:35520
*************************END RTP Perf Log**************************


Signature updated on Sun Apr 15 2012 11:58:52
Product Version: 3.0.8410.0
Service version: 3.0.8410.0
Engine Version: 1.1.8202.0
AS Signature Version: 1.123.1813.0
AV Signature Version: 1.123.1813.0
*****************************************************************
2012-04-15T15:58:53.031Z Process scan started.
Signature updated via MMPC on Sun Apr 15 2012 11:59:01
*****************************************************************

-----------------------------------------------------------------
System Center 2012 Endpoint Protection (1F383481-F70E-4E7A-8B69-C4B4A23928E3) Service Log
Started On Sun Apr 15 2012 12:36:06
*****************************************************Cache stats*********
No. of buckets -> 53
Each Bucket has max capacity of -> 128 entries
number of Entries is 0
Number of invalid entries is 0
Number of Inserts issued is 0
Number of replaces issued is 0
Number of Insert failures is 0
Number of lookups is 0
Number of misses is 0
Number of false fast lookups is 0
Number of invalidations is 0                                         ▼
◄                                                                   ►
```

7. You can continue to shift through the log by hitting *F3* to jump to the next entry that contains the word **updated**. As we remediated an issue with the Microsoft Updates EULA and forced an update, we should expect to see a change in the latest entry. If the client was able to reach Microsoft Updates for a definition, your latest entry should read **Signature updated via MicrosoftUpdateServer**. Refer to the following screenshot:

```
MPLog-04152012-112408 - Notepad                                    _|□|×|
File  Edit  Format  View  Help
Engine Version: 1.1.8304.0                                            ▲
AS Signature Version: 1.125.1716.0
AV Signature Version: 1.125.1716.0
*****************************************************************
2012-05-12T15:15:42.343Z Process scan started.
Signature updated via MicrosoftUpdateServer on Sat May 12 2012 11:15:43
*****************************************************************
2012-05-12T15:15:52.640Z Process scan completed.
2012-05-12T23:14:49.500Z Task(SignatureUpdate -ScheduleJob -RestrictPrivileges) launche
2012-05-12T23:19:34.843Z AutoPurgeworker triggered with dwwork=0x3
2012-05-12T23:19:34.843Z Product supports installmode: 2
2012-05-12T23:19:35.046Z Detection State: Finished(0) Failed(0) CriticalFailed(0) Addit
2012-05-13T07:14:49.390Z Task(SignatureUpdate -ScheduleJob -RestrictPrivileges) launche
-----------------------------------------------------------------
System Center 2012 Endpoint Protection (1F383481-F70E-4E7A-8B69-C4B4A23928E3) Service L
Started On Sun May 27 2012 11:13:30
*****************************************************Cache stats****** ▼
◄                                                                   ►
```

8. If every effort has failed so far and you simply need to get the client up-to-date for the immediate future, it is possible to manually download a complete definition file from Microsoft's security portal. Open Internet Explorer and follow the instructions for manual download at this site: `http://www.microsoft.com/security/portal/Definitions/HowToForeFront.aspx`. Refer to the following screenshot:

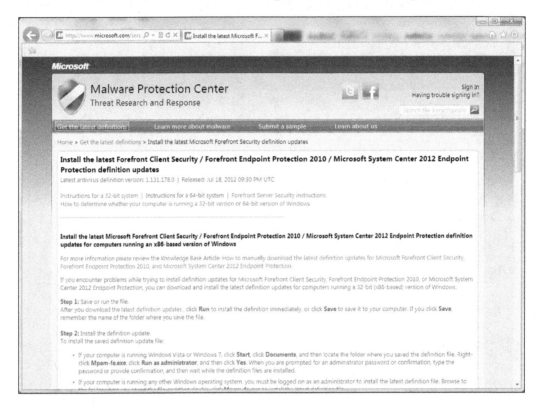

How it works...

Due to the redundancy that Microsoft has built into the SCEP client by allowing SCEP definitions to be pulled from multiple sources, the client is very good at keeping itself up-to-date. As the client does not, by default, report from where it obtained an update (only the version number of its current definition), it is not always immediately apparent that a prescribed definition update source has failed.

By logging into a client and reviewing its MPLog, we can surmise when a client failed over to secondary update methods. If many of your clients are doing so, it's likely that a configuration setting has changed. It is recommended that you review the component status messages for the SUP component and verify the configuration of your Automatic Deployment Rules for SCEP.

Fixing SCCM client health issues

Anyone reading this book who has administered any of SCCM 2012's predecessors will likely agree that the biggest headache was keeping your installed client base healthy; especially when working with SCCM clients running on Windows XP, which had a nasty habit of corrupting their WMI data.

With SCCM 2012, Microsoft has addressed many of issues with the inclusion of two monitoring components, Client Activity and Client Check. As an SCEP administrator, your ability to monitor malware activity is directly affected by the overall health status of SCCM clients.

This recipe will walk you through the process for utilizing Client Activity and Client Check to resolve some common issues. To illustrate this point, we will be working on workstation which seems to be no longer communicating with SCCM.

Getting ready

To complete this recipe, you will need to be using an account that has SCCM administrator privileges.

How to do it...

1. Log in to your SCCM CAS server and launch your SCCM 2012 management console.

2. Navigate to `Monitoring\Overview\Client Status\Client Activity` in the collection field; click on **browse**, and select **All Systems**. Click on the word **Inactive** to create a node which contains a list of all the clients that have been flagged inactive; your console should automatically switch to viewing this list. Refer to the following screenshot:

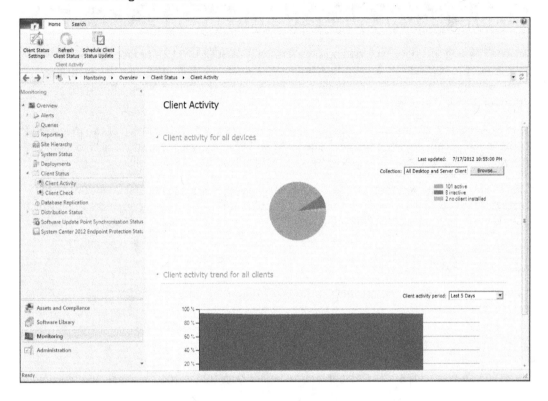

3. By entering the name of the workstation in the search bar, we can quickly determine if it is in this list or not. If the workstation is in this list, then it has not communicated with SCCM in over seven days.

4. With inactive clients, it is always worth the effort to find the user of this workstation to check if they have simply gone on vacation and left their workstation powered down. To find out to whom a workstation belongs, right-click on the computer object and select **Properties**. Locate the **Last Logon User Name** properties. You can also view the last **Logon Time Stamp (UTC)** here as well. Refer to the following screenshot:

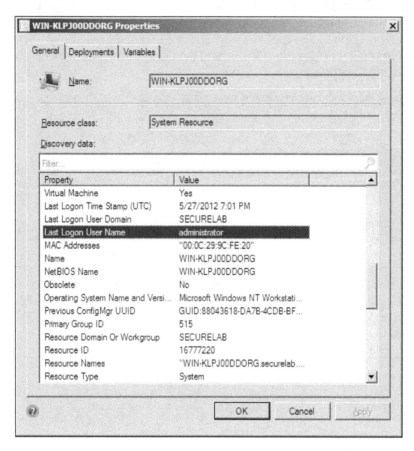

5. If you have reached this point and determined that the workstation has not sent a heartbeat to SCCM more than seven days and no one has logged into it for the same amount of time, you can be fairly sure it's simply turned off. To verify this, you should attempt to ping the hostname (provided your firewall policy allows for pinging).

6. One important thing to know in this scenario is: does your SCCM server have the clear install flag maintenance task enabled and if so, what is the threshold (the default is 21 days)? If you are using the clear install flag task, then as long as the PC is booted back up before the threshold is reached, everything be fine. If the PC will remains off longer than the clear install flag threshold, then SCCM will consider the workstation to have no SCCM client and the client will likely need to be redeployed to resolve the issue. To check your organization's current clear install flag setting, navigate to `\Administration\Overview\Site Configuration\Sites`, click on the **Settings** button at the top of the UI, and then select **Site Maintenance**. Refer to the following screenshot:

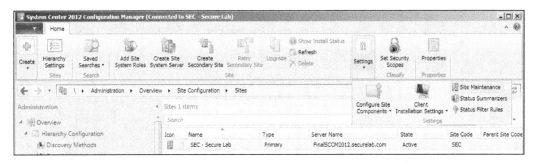

7. Next, we will be taking a look at the dashboard for client check, which pertains to SCCM 2012 abilities to self-heal many client issues. Navigate to `Monitoring\ Overview\Client Status\Client Check`, click on **client check failed** to bring up a node that lists all of the clients that have failed their client check. Refer to the following screenshot:

8. Browse the list for any workstations that you suspect have not been reporting their SCEP data. If you do find any of these machines, the first step in remediation is usually to attempt to redeploy the client. To do so, right-click on the computer object and select **Install Client**.

9. On the **Installation Options** page of the **Install Configuration Manager client Wizard**, make sure to select the option **Always install the client software**. This will reinstall the client even if the workstation already has one (albeit a broken client). Refer to the following screenshot:

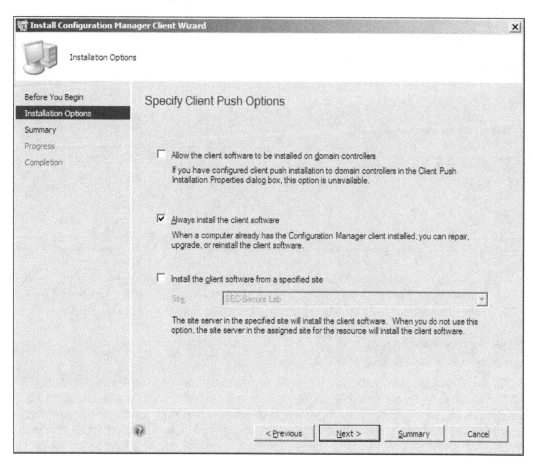

10. After you complete the wizard, you will see a summary completion page. This does not mean that the client was successfully reinstalled, just that the client push process was initiated. To view the current status of the client push, navigate to `Monitoring\Overview\Reporting\Reports` and execute the **Client Push Installation** details report. Refer to the following screenshot:

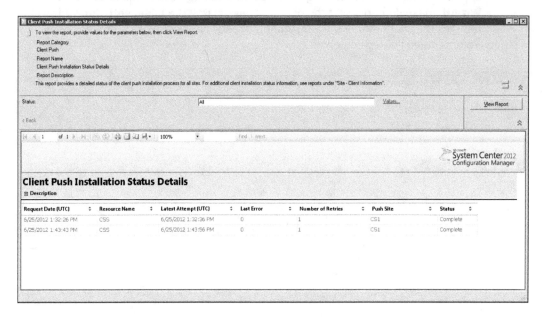

11. If the client redeployment fails, check that the target PC is online and that the correct firewall ports are opened for SCCM client push. You will also want to verify that the service account used for client push is a local administrator of the target system.

How it works...

SCCM uses its Client Activity and Client Check components to help administrators monitor their client base. While the Client Check component can deal with many common issues, such as remediating some **Windows Management Instrumentation** (**WMI**) issues, or verifying the operation and startup type for typical Windows services the client needs, it will not be able to fix every issue that occurs with an SCCM client. Sometimes the only choice is to redeploy the client.

If redeployment fails, the next step is to make sure the client still meets the minimum requirements for SCCM. One common configuration change that affects clients is closing WMI from remote systems or disabling the SMB ports. Also, if client pushes should fail, it's a good idea to verify that the service account for client installation has not been disabled.

Resolving false positives

Although SCEP is known for having a fairly low rate of false positives, they will sometimes occur. One common issue that many organizations deal with is the fact that both, DameWare and VNC, are flagged as malicious remote control software in the SCEP definition file. This was done, because a number of Trojans have been known to contain elements of these products.

In this recipe, we will be removing a false positive for DameWare by configuring our policy to overlook it.

Getting ready

For this recipe, you will need to utilize an account that has at least the SCEP administrator role assigned to it.

How to do it...

Follow these steps:

1. Log into your SCCM CAS server and launch your SCCM 2012 management console.
2. Navigate to `Assets and Compliance\Overview\Endpoint Protection\Antimalware Policies`, select a policy that applies to the workstation or server that is experiencing the false positive, right-click on the policy, and select **properties**.
3. Select **Threat Overrides** from the ribbon on the left-hand side and click on the **set** button.
4. Next, click on the browse button and the **Browse Threat Name** window should pop up.
5. In the **Threat name** field, type in `dameware` and click on **Find**. Select **RemoteAccess:Win32/DameWareMiniRemote** from the list and click on **OK**, as shown in the following screenshot:

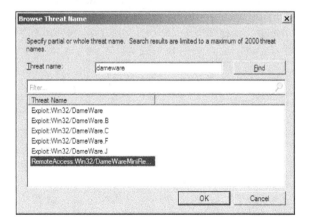

6. You should now be back at the **Configure Setting** window; hit the drop-down arrow next to **Override action**, and select **Allow**.

7. Click on the **Add** button and DameWare should now appear in the list of overrides. Click on the **OK** button to close the window.

8. Click on the **OK** button again to close the policy editor.

9. The changes to the policy will replicate to your workstations and servers on their normal policy refresh cycle (one hour by default).

How it works...

SCEP uses a system of threat overrides to deal with false positives. An override can change the default action that SCEP takes for any piece of malware listed in its policy, so overrides should be used sparingly. A misconfigured override could leave your clients vulnerable.

If you were performing this pre-emptively, then no further action would be required. If, however, you were performing these steps after detection, it may be necessary for you to de-quarantine the files affected or re-install the application.

De-quarantining is done at the local client level from the **History** tab of the client UI. It is important to remember that the default for the number of days files will reside in the quarantine is 14 days. After that period, files will be purged and cannot be restored.

False positives for in-house developed applications:

In the example provided in this recipe, a false positive was remediated for a specific commercially available product that Microsoft considers suspicious and which has its own clearly defined listing in the SCEP definition file that can be overridden. However, it is also possible for an in-house developed application to be falsely identified as malware, because it shares some similarities in its code with an actual piece of malware.

In this case, you could choose to create an override for the malware that SCEP believes your application to be. This would in turn create a potential security hole, because if an instance of the genuine malware made it onto your network, your PCs would not be protected. A much better option is to go through the process of submitting the affected software to Microsoft for remediation.

This can be done going to the Microsoft Malware Protection website and submitting a sample and selecting the option, **I believe this file should not be detected as malware**. Refer to the following screenshot:

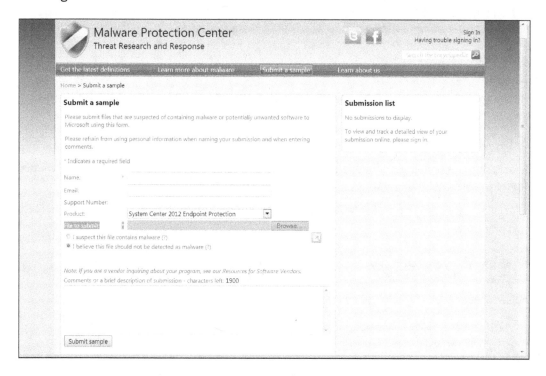

Dealing with infections that SCEP cannot resolve

There is no such thing as an anti-malware product that is 100% percent effective against all malware. So, it's very likely that during its life span in your environment, SCEP will fail you at least once. This recipe will guide you through the process of dealing with such a failure and helping to ensure that the infection does not spread to other machines.

In this recipe, you'll be working with a scenario, where SCEP has detected a piece of malware and reports that it has successfully removed it, but unfortunately after a short time, the malware comes back and is re-detected by SCEP. No one has been logged into the PC during this outbreak, which removes the possibility that a user is re-downloading an attachment or re-installing a rouge program, after each infection.

Typically what this kind of behavior would indicate is that there is actually more malware on the PC than what SCEP can detect. The malware that is going undetected is likely a Trojan downloader, which is a piece of malware that hides on a PC and downloads other payloads from a web server.

To combat this, we will be performing what is referred to as an offline or a boot scan. To do this, we will be using Microsoft's free Windows Defender Offline scan tool (which is available online as a free download). It's important to note that this is the same function you would perform if you looked up at malware detection event in the SCCM console and the malware status stated that remediation status was **Offline Scan Required**.

Getting ready

Before you can begin the procedure, you'll need to download the latest version of the offline scanner tool.

```
http://go.microsoft.com/fwlink/?LinkID=232461
```

It is strongly recommended that you download and run the utility to create the bootable media from PC that is not the one with the infection.

You will need either a CDR or USB drive that you are willing to reformat to complete this procedure.

How to do it...

Follow these steps:

1. Double-click on `mssstool.exe` to begin the process. The Windows Defender Offline tool should launch. Agree to the EULA and click on **Next**, as shown in the following screenshot:

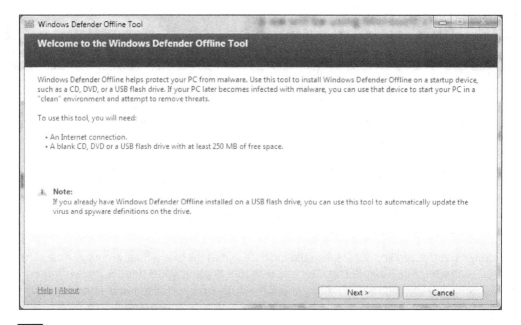

2. Select the type of media you wish to use for this procedure, as shown in the following screenshot:

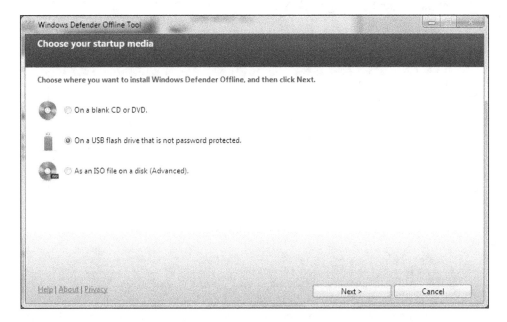

3. If you are using an USB drive, then agree to the warning message pertaining to reformatting, as shown in the following screenshot:

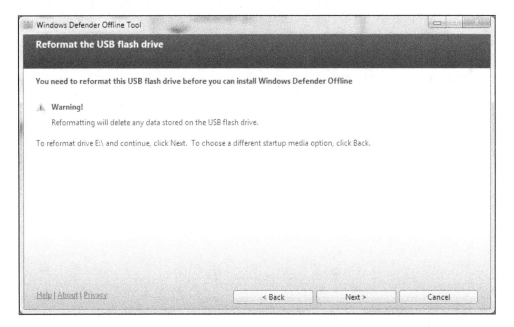

4. Next, the utility will automatically download the latest version of image file, format the media, and write the image to the media. This can take several minutes to complete, as shown in the following screenshot:

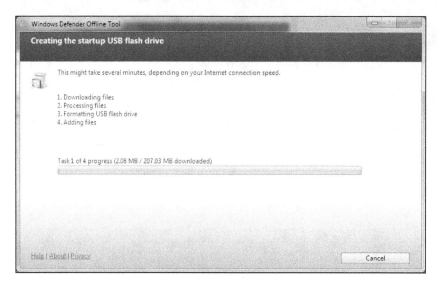

5. Once the process is complete, you'll be presented with a screen outlining the next steps, which essentially consist of booting the infected PC to the USB drive we have just created. Once the PC is booted, you'll be presented with the option to do a full or quick scan. It is recommended to do a full scan in this situation, since if you've had to go to the length of doing an offline scan, the PC could be infected with multitude of malware. Refer to the following screenshot:

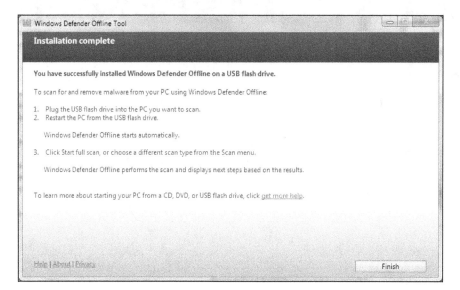

How it works...

Under the hood, **Windows Defender Offline** scanner is essentially the same thing as your SCEP client. It has the same engine and definition files that you use on your desktop. What gives it the ability to combat malware that SCEP couldn't remove is the fact that you're booting into a sandboxed environment. The only things that are allowed to load when you boot to offline scanner media are the components of the OS that are needed to run the scanner and nothing else.

Other standalone scanners:

In addition to the Windows Defender utility covered in this recipe, there are several other products that you might choose to utilize in combating malware that SCEP could not deal with.

I would recommend Malware Bytes, which is free and highly effective.

```
http://www.malwarebytes.org/
```

9
Building an SCCM 2012 Lab

In this chapter, we will cover:

▸ Installing SCCM 2012 and SCEP in a standalone environment

Introduction

This chapter consists of a single recipe, which lays out a quick and easy procedure for setting up a small single server SCCM environment, which can be used to evaluate SCEP. This recipe will allow you to quickly get an SCCM/SCEP lab up and running, to examine the products for yourself and conduct a proof of concept.

There's no planning or design decisions taken into account here, just the basic steps are laid out from beginning to end.

Installing SCCM 2012 and SCEP in a standalone environment

Very few organizations would ever consider deploying something such as SCCM 2012 and SCEP in their production environment without kicking the tires first. Typically, what's done long before a decision is made to buy the product is something called a **Proof of Concept** (**POC**). During a POC, SCCM is installed in a lab environment that has its own AD domain and subnet.

It's always a good idea in the lab to have some workstations that are built off your corporate standardized image. This will allow you to deploy the SCCM and SCEP clients and give you the chance to verify that the clients are not going to adversely affect your applications or hamper the user experience.

Conducting a POC in a lab is not quite the same thing as building out SCCM and SCEP in a development environment; if you work for a medium to large-scale organization, a single SCCM server in a standalone primary site configuration would not be very representative of your production topology. On the other hand, there probably isn't any reason that a small-scale company couldn't just keep their SCCM/SCEP POC environment up to use as the development environment.

Getting ready

Before completing this recipe, you will need to have access to a lab environment. The lab should have its own AD domain and therefore, requires at least a single Windows 2008 R2 level domain controller. In order to prevent any bleed into your production environment, it's advisable to put the lab on its own VLAN or at least a separate subnet.

Virtualization is, typically, the way to go with a lab environment; just ensure that any virtual machines created for the lab meet the minimum SCCM 2012 requirements.

The recipe assumes that you've installed Windows 2008 R2 on your server and have joined the server to the domain. You will need to have enterprise admin-level access to the domain as changes to the schema will be needed.

In terms of hardware requirements, a server (or VM) that has at least a dual core CPU, 8 GB of RAM and 60 GB of available disk space should suffice for this lab.

How to do it...

1. Begin by creating the following service and user accounts with the prescribed permissions. It is not necessary to use the same user names I have, but for simplicity, I recommend you to do so. You will also need a user account with Domain Administrator privileges and an account with rights to modify the AD schema.

    1. Client Push: This is the domain user that will be used to push SCCM clients and therefore, must have local admin privileges on all the PCs that will be targeted for client installation

    2. SCCM admin: This is the domain user with local admin privileges for the SCCM server

2. Next, we will be creating the **Systems Management** container within `Active` directory. To do this, log in with a domain admin account and open **ADSI Edit**. Expand the root level object and locate the folder titled `CN=System`. Right click on **CN=System**, select **New**, and then select **Object**. Refer to the following screenshot:

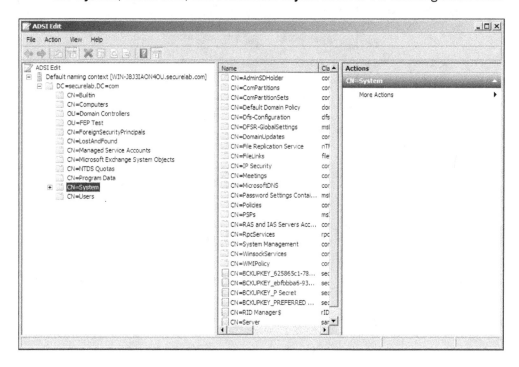

3. Select **container** in the **Create Object** window and click on **Next**. In the field for **Value**, enter `System Management`, and click on **Next**. Then, click on **Finish** to complete the wizard. Refer to the following screenshot:

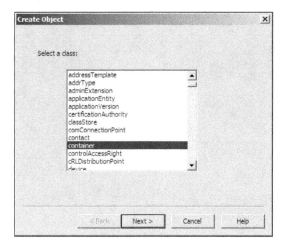

4. Next, we will be granting your SCCM server's computer account permissions to the **System Management** container we just created. First open **Active Directory Users and Computers**, and then click on **View** and select **Advanced Features**. Expand the **System** container and locate the **System Management** object. Right-click on it and select **Delegate Control**, as shown in the following screenshot:

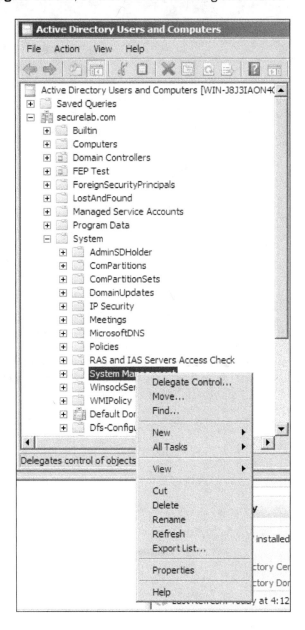

5. The **Delegation of Control Wizard** should appear, then click on **Next** on the welcome page. Next, click on **Add** and the **Select Users, Computers, or Groups** window should pop up. Click on the **object types** button and click on the checkbox next to **Computers**. Click on **OK** to return to the previous window. Now you should be able to enter the machine name of your SCCM server and then click to check names. Click **OK** to close the **Select Users, Computers**, or **Groups** window.

6. You should now be looking at the **Delegation of Control Wizard** again, and your SCCM server should be present in the list. Click on **Next** to proceed.

7. In the **Tasks to Delegate** window, select the **Create a custom task to delegate** option and click on **Next**, as shown in the following screenshot:

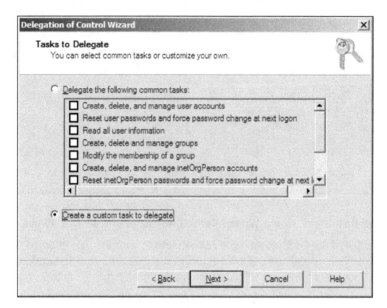

8. On the **Active Directory Object Type** page, select the top option, **This folder, existing objects in this folder and creation of new objects in this folder**, and click on **Next**. Refer to the following screenshot:

9. On the **Permissions** page, select **General**, **Property-Specific**, and **Creation-deletion of specific child objects** and then under **Permissions** enable **Full Control**, as shown in the following screenshot:

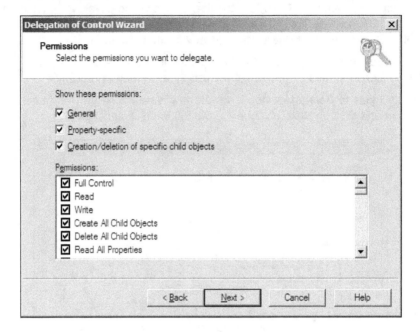

10. Click on **Next** to review the **Wizard Completion** page and click on **Finish** to close it out.

11. The next step will be to extend the AD schema in your lab. It's important to note that if your lab has already had the AD schema extended in order to support SCCM 2007, you will not have to repeat this step, as the schema extensions have not changed.

12. While still logged into the domain controller, browse to your SCCM installation media. Right-click on SMSSetup\Bin\x64\Extadsch.exe and run it as an administrator. Once the process is complete, you can verify success by taking a look at ExtADSch.log, which should be on the root of C:\.

13. Next, you will need to install .NET 3.5.1 with WCF activation on the SCCM server. From **Server Manager**, select **Features**, then click on **Add features**, and choose .**NET Framework 3.5.1 along with WCF activation**. When presented with option to **Add required role services**, do so. Click on **Next** and **Next** again to complete the wizard. Confirm afterwards in **Server Manager** whether the following IIS components have all been installed:

   ❑ Common HTTP Features

   ❑ Static Content

   ❑ Default Document

   ❑ Directory Browsing

- ❏ HTTP Errors
- ❏ HTTP Redirection
- ❏ Application Development
- ❏ ASP.NET
- ❏ .NET Extensibility
- ❏ ASP
- ❏ ISAPI Extensions
- ❏ ISAPI Filters
- ❏ Health and Diagnostics
- ❏ HTTP logging
- ❏ Logging tools
- ❏ Request Monitor
- ❏ Tracing
- ❏ Security
- ❏ Basic Authentication
- ❏ Windows Authentication
- ❏ URL Authorization
- ❏ Request Filtering
- ❏ IP and Domain Restrictions
- ❏ Performance
- ❏ Static Content Compression
- ❏ Management Tools
- ❏ IIS Management Console
- ❏ IIS Management Scripts and Tools
- ❏ Management Service
- ❏ IIS 6 Management Compatibility
- ❏ IIS 6 Metabase Compatibility
- ❏ IIS 6 WMI Compatibility
- ❏ IIS 6 Scripting Tools
- ❏ IIS 6 Management Console

14. While you are still in the server management console, you will want to go ahead and add the **Background Intelligent Transfer Service** (**BITS**) and **Remote Differential Compression**. These two options can be found under features.

15. Next, we will install .NET Framework 4. This will need to be downloaded from Microsoft. The wizard is very straightforward, simply run it on your SCCM server and click on **Next** until it completes.

16. The next step is to install SQL server 2008. SCCM 2012 has very specific version requirements for SQL, so make sure you are installing a version that is fully supported. I generally stick with SQL Server 2008 R2 with SP1 and with a minimum of Cumulative Update 6 for the labs I've built. Refer to this technet page to see all of the versions that can be used with SCCM 2012: `http://technet.microsoft. com/en-us/library/gg682077.aspx#BKMK_SupConfigSQLSrvReq`

17. For the lab, we will be installing SQL directly onto the primary site server. Launch the SQL installation from `setup.exe` contained in your SQL Server 2008 installation media. For the purposes of this lab, you do not need to concern yourself too much with the configuration; simply proceed through the wizard until you get to the installation page, make sure to choose **New SQL Server Standalone Installation** or **Add features to an existing installation**.

18. Once all of the support files are installed, you will be presented with the **Feature Selection** page. Click on the **Select All** button and proceed through the wizard until it is completed.

19. After SQL is installed, install the correct service pack for your version and then install the Cumulative Update. Reboot server before proceeding to the next step.

20. Now it's finally time to install SCCM 2012. To begin, insert the CD or mount the ISO file and the installation wizard should appear. Refer to the following screenshot:

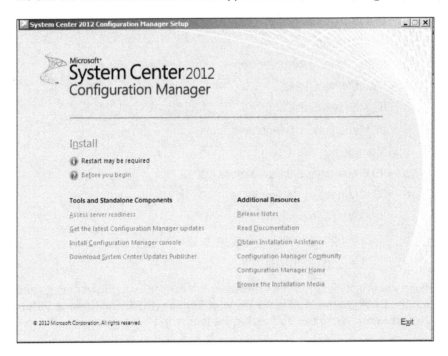

21. Review the posted information on **Before You Begin** and then click on **Next** to proceed, as shown in the following screenshot:

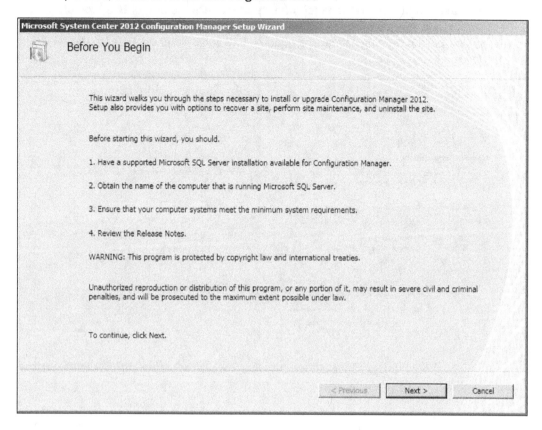

Microsoft System Center 2012 Configuration Manager Setup Wizard

Before You Begin

This wizard walks you through the steps necessary to install or upgrade Configuration Manager 2012. Setup also provides you with options to recover a site, perform site maintenance, and uninstall the site.

Before starting this wizard, you should.

1. Have a supported Microsoft SQL Server installation available for Configuration Manager.

2. Obtain the name of the computer that is running Microsoft SQL Server.

3. Ensure that your computer systems meet the minimum system requirements.

4. Review the Release Notes.

WARNING: This program is protected by copyright law and international treaties.

Unauthorized reproduction or distribution of this program, or any portion of it, may result in severe civil and criminal penalties, and will be prosecuted to the maximum extent possible under law.

To continue, click Next.

< Previous   Next >   Cancel

22. On the page titled **Getting Started**, you will be selecting the topology for this installation. As we are just putting together a lab, we will choose the first option **Install a Configuration Manager primary site**. Check the box for **Use Typical for a stand-alone primary site**. Click on **Next** to proceed and then, click on **OK** on the pop-up warning concerning to add a CAS server later on. Refer to the following screenshot:

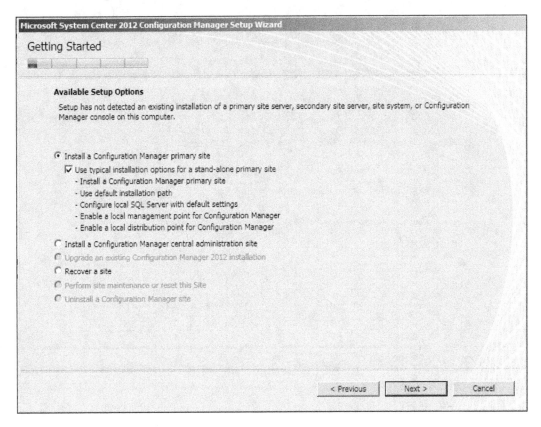

23. On the **Product Key** page, you can either enter your product key or choose to install the product as an evaluation. Click on **Next** to proceed, as shown in the following screenshot:

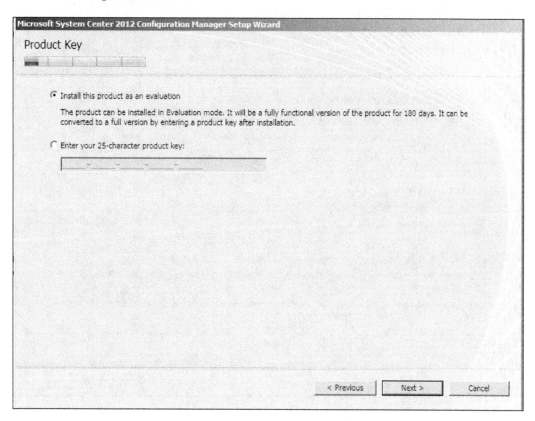

24. The next page will present you with the EULA, agree to it, and click on **Next** to proceed, as shown in the following screenshot:

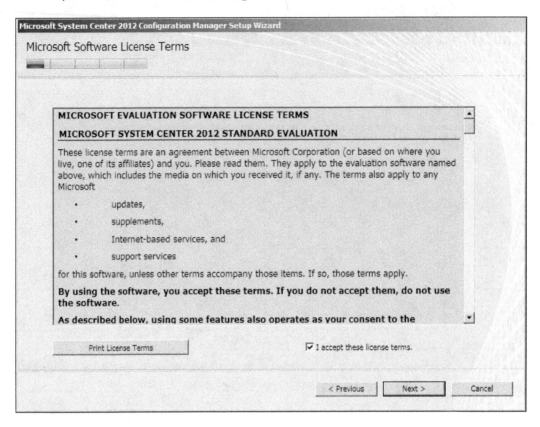

25. The next page has more EULAs to agree to for additional products that will be installed during the process, accept them, and click on **Next** to proceed. Refer to the following screenshot:

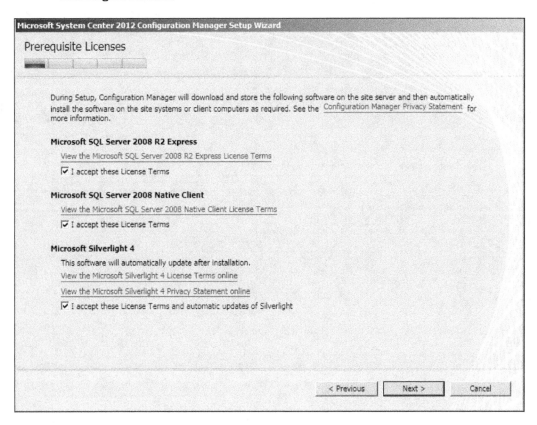

26. On the **Prerequisites Download** page, give the wizard a file location to download some data for the installation process. Click on **Next** to proceed, as shown in the following screenshot:

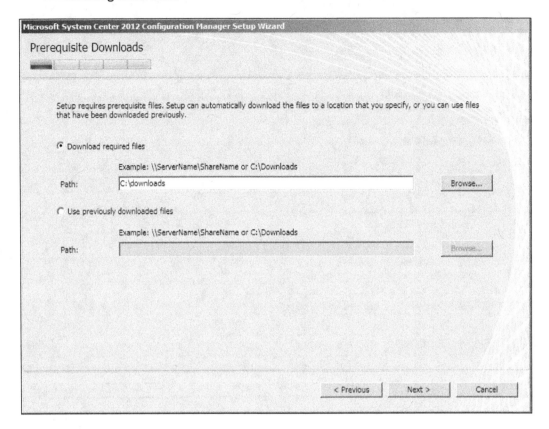

27. Next, we have the **Site and Installation Settings** page, where we need to define **Site code**, **Site name**, and **Installation folder**. One thing to remember: if this environment had SCCM 2007 in it before, do not reuse the same **Site code**. You will need to come up with a new one. Click on the **Next** button to move forward, as shown in the following screenshot:

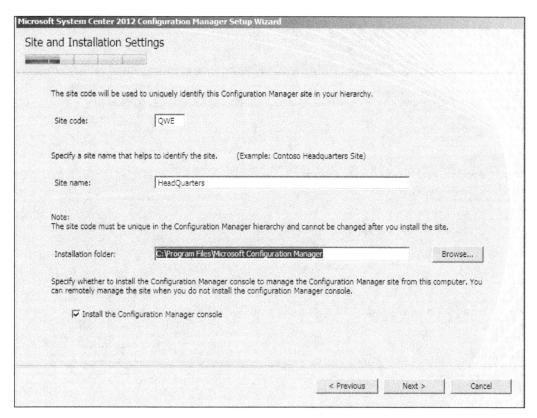

28. Next, you will be presented with the option to join the end user experience program, make your selection, and click on **Next** to proceed, as shown in the following screenshot:

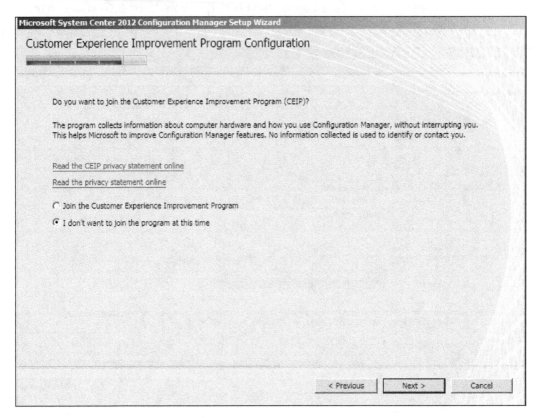

Microsoft System Center 2012 Configuration Manager Setup Wizard

Customer Experience Improvement Program Configuration

Do you want to join the Customer Experience Improvement Program (CEIP)?

The program collects information about computer hardware and how you use Configuration Manager, without interrupting you. This helps Microsoft to improve Configuration Manager features. No information collected is used to identify or contact you.

Read the CEIP privacy statement online

Read the privacy statement online

○ Join the Customer Experience Improvement Program

⦿ I don't want to join the program at this time

< Previous   Next >   Cancel

29. The next page is the **Settings Summary** page, review what you've done so far, and if you're content with your selections, click on **Next** to proceed, as shown in the following screenshot:

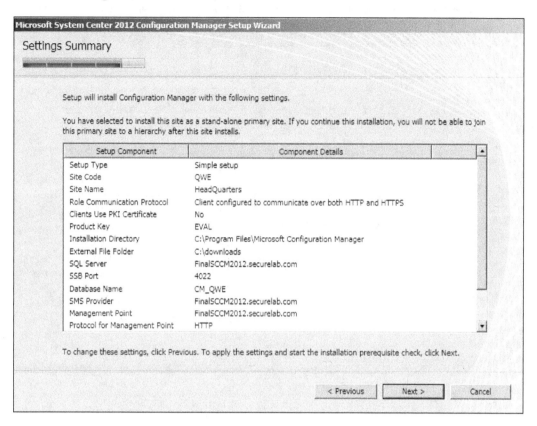

30. Now the **Prerequisite Check** will run. This will verify that you installed all the prerequisites correctly. If there are no issues, click on the **Begin Install** button to proceed. If there are any errors, click on the **More Information** button to learn what steps need to be taken to remediate them, as shown in the following screenshot:

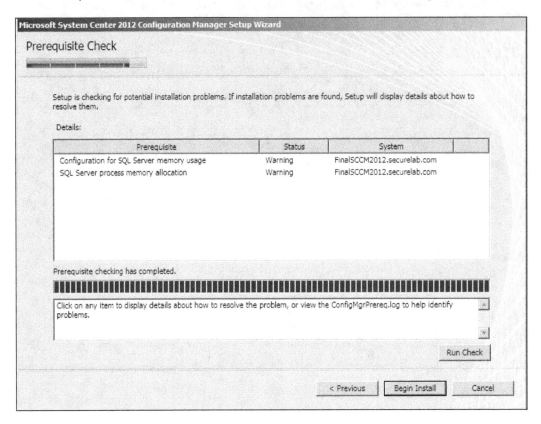

31. The installation will run for some time, perhaps 15 minutes or more. If everything is processed correctly, at the end, you will be presented with many happy green check marks. Click on **Next** to close the wizard, as shown in the following screenshot:

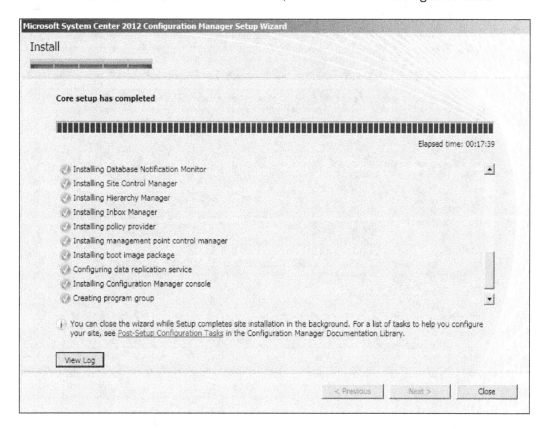

32. At this point, you could proceed with enabling the Primary Site's Endpoint Protection role, but if you want the lab to cover both the server-side and the client-side aspects of SCEP, you will need to deploy some clients. To do this, you will first need to establish some boundaries in SCCM and then a method of discovery. For this lab environment, I recommend utilizing at least the Active Directory System Discovery method and an AD Site boundary.

33. Next, you will need to set up the **Client Installation** properties in `Administration\ Overview\Site Configuration\Sites`. On the **Accounts** properties tab, enter the **Client Push** service account we created in step one. Refer to the following screenshot:

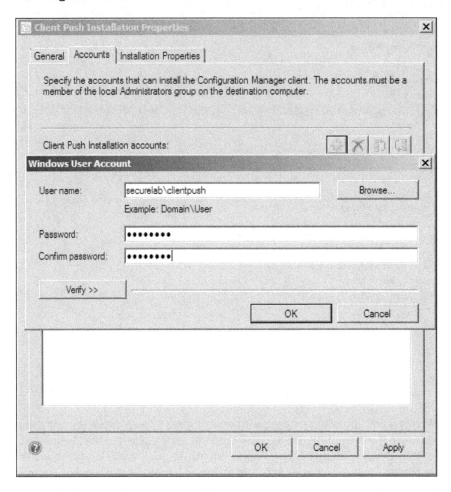

34. Once the AD system discovery has completed for the first time, you should start to see some machine names populating the **All Systems** collection. You can install the SCCM client on them by right-clicking on them and selecting **Install client**.

How it works...

The installation of SCCM has been greatly streamlined in the 2012 version compared to earlier versions of the product, but still there is a fair amount of prep work that must be done beforehand. Implementing the prerequisites correctly will help to ensure a smooth installation of SCCM itself.

Once SCCM is up and stable, you can then follow the recipes in *Chapter 2, Planning and Rolling Installation*, to implement SCEP.

Appendix

With the previous version of SCEP (Forefront Endpoint Protection 2010), many organizations opted to install the FEP 2010 Security Management Pack for SCOM, because it added the ability to have real-time reporting. As SCEP has the real-time reporting capabilities natively, this is not as necessary with the current version.

However, there could be other motivating factors that would cause an organization to still choose to install the newly updated System Center Security Monitoring Pack for Endpoint Protection, such as the way monitoring responsibilities have been allocated in your organization, or you may be using an SEM appliance, which connects to SCOM and want to have virus alerts filter up into the SEM.

Integrating SCEP with SCOM 2012

In order to install the System Center Security Monitoring Pack for Endpoint Protection, you will need to use an account with administrator access to SCOM. You will also need to download the management pack, which is available at the following URL:

```
http://www.microsoft.com/en-us/download/details.aspx?id=9754
```

Now, follow these steps:

1. Begin by logging into your SCOM management server and unpacking the MSI, which you downloaded from Microsoft's website. To do so, double-click on `fep2010 security mp.msi` and agree to EULA. Do not worry that the management pack we just downloaded has FEP in the title; this MP works for SCEP as well. Refer to the following screenshot:

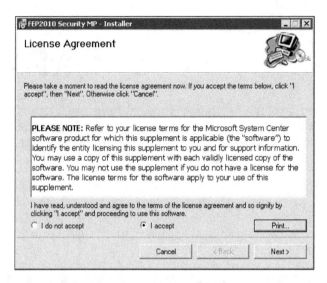

2. Next, select a destination path for the files to unpack to. Whether you stick with the default or choose your own location is up to you. Either way make sure to copy the path, as you will need it in a later step. Refer to the following screenshot:

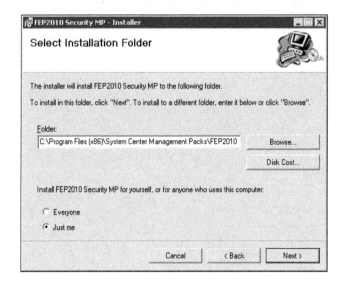

3. Now just click on the **Install** button and wait for the task to complete, as shown in the following screenshot:

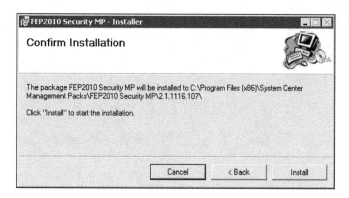

4. Now you will need to open the SCOM management console, and select the **Administration** tab. Locate the **Management Packs** object and then right-click on it. Select the option for **Import Management Packs**, as shown in the following screenshot:

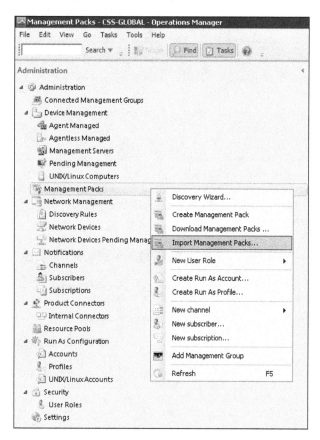

5. The **Import Management Packs** wizard should appear. Next, click on the **Add** button, as shown in the following screenshot:

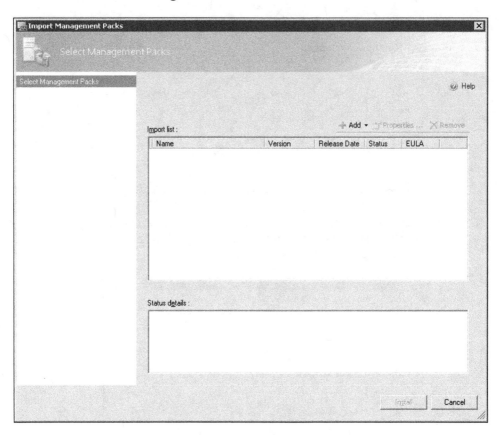

6. You'll be prompted with an **Online Catalog Connection** dialog box, as we've already downloaded the management pack. Now, click on **No** to proceed, as shown in the following screenshot:

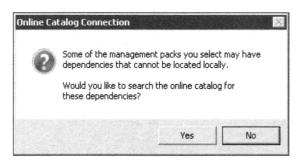

7. You'll then be presented with a window that allows you to browse to the location
    for which we unpacked the files to in step 2. The first file you'll need to pick is
    `Microsoft.FEPS.Libary.mp`. Then, click on the **Open** button to proceed, as
    shown in the following screenshot:

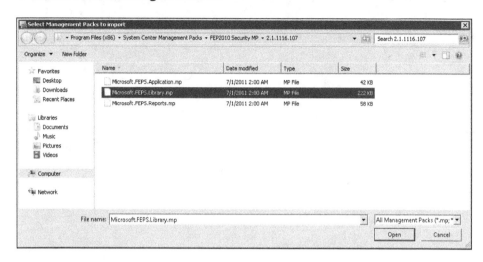

8. You will be brought back to the **Import Management Packs** wizard. If you've selected
    the correct file, then you'll see a green check next to the filename. You'll need to click
    on the **Add** button again and repeat the process for the other two files in the folder,
    `Microsoft.FEPS.Application.mp` and `Microsoft.FEPS.Reports.mp`. Once
    you've added all three `.mp` files, you can then click on the **Install** button, as shown in
    the following screenshot:

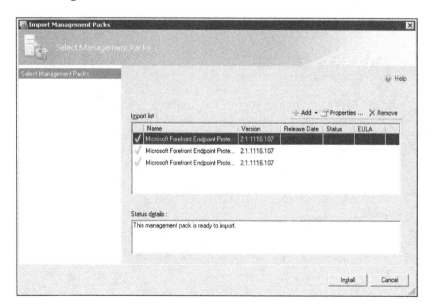

9. The import process will likely take a few minutes, but once it's complete, you should see the following screenshot:

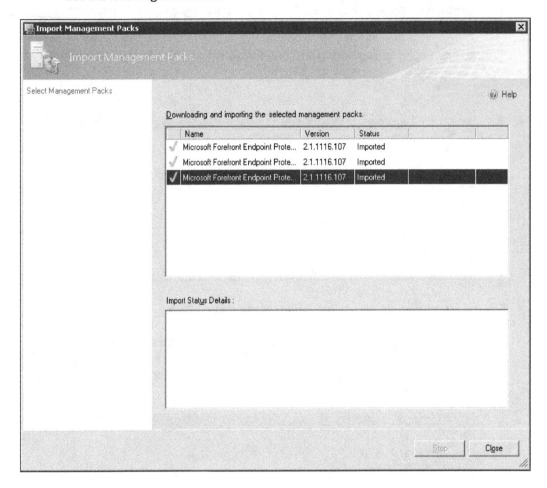

10. Click on the **Close** button to complete the import procedure.

The procedure in this recipe will only import the management pack into your SCOM 2012 environment, in order. For clients, to start sending SCEP related data to SCOM, they will also need to have the SCOM client deployed to them. In other words, the SCOM Management Pack collects data directly from the Endpoint clients themselves, rather than pulling data out of your SCCM 2012 server.

As such, there is a lot of overlap between SCCM 2012 with SCEP enabled and a SCOM server with the Endpoint Protection Management pack installed. Therefore, it's recommended that you only use the Management Pack if you have a good reason for doing so.

Client deployment checklists

The client deployment checklist is provided in the following table:

Client Deployment Checklists	Notes
Has your SCCM 2012 been scaled out to support the number of SCEP clients you're intending to deploy?	
Have you implemented enough distribution points to supply SCEP definitions on a daily basis without impacting network performance?	
Have you disseminated enough information about the upcoming deployment to technical staff and end users?	
Have you fully tested your legacy AV removal procedure? If it's not absolutely 100% effective, what is the expected percentage of failure?	
Have you created a procedure for dealing with failed SCEP installations?	
Have you created and tested SCEP policies for all the system types that your deployment targets?	
Is there an existing channel of communication for end users that experience performance issues after SCEP is deployed?	
Has there been a maintenance window created for deploying SCEP to Windows servers?	
Is your help desk ready to respond to an increased number of virus detections?	
Have you grouped your deployment targets into logical groups of systems that will allow for deploying in a phased manner?	

List of SCEP logfiles

You can find the SCEP client logfiles in the following location:

- `%allusersprofile%\Microsoft\Microsoft Antimalware\Support` contains the SCEP client operational logs, which include:
  - `MPDetection-XXXXXXXX-XXXXXX.log` that logs information pertaining to malware detections
  - `MPLog-XXXXXXXX-XXXXXX.log` that logs all of the SCEP clients activity to include definition updates, malware detections, and the raising of behavior monitoring alerts

- ▶ `%allusersprofile%\Microsoft\Microsoft Security Client\Support`
  contains the SCEP client installation logs, which include:
    - ❑ `EppSetup.log`
    - ❑ `MSSecurityClient_Setup_epp_install.log`
    - ❑ `MSSecurityClient_Setup_epp_install.log`
    - ❑ `MSSecurityClient_Setup_mp_ambits_install.log`

The primary log for client installation troubleshooting efforts will be `EppSetup.log`.

Using Windows Intune Endpoint Protection

Windows Intune is a subscription-based management solution that utilizes Microsoft cloud-based services to manage Windows-based PCs wherever they may be. It is primarily intended to provide all of the management power that SCCM has to offer to small to medium-sized organizations that do not wish to implement on-premises servers.

One of the features it provides is Endpoint Protection. The anti-malware client used by Intune is identical to the one SCEP uses, with the exception that Intune client reports back to Microsoft's cloud services.

If you have not tried Intune before, Microsoft offers a free 30-day trial to grant you access to all of its features. This recipe walks you through the process of installing the Intune client, enabling Endpoint Protection from the console, and verifying that your Intune client reports back to your Intune console when a virus is detected. The recipe assumes that you have signed up for a trial or own a subscription to Intune.

If you have not signed up for Intune, a free trial is offered on the following link:

`http://www.microsoft.com/en-us/windows/windowsintune/pc-management.aspx`

You will need to have administrator access to the Intune console and local administrator permissions on the PC you're performing this recipe on.

Now, perform the following steps:

1. Begin by logging into the Intune console at `https://manage.microsoft.com/WindowsIntune` from the PC that you are testing with. Click on the scroll-shaped icon on the left-hand side of the console to access the **Policy** page. Refer to the following screenshot:

2. Next, click on the **Add Policy** button to create a new policy. The **Create New Policy** wizard should appear within your browser. Select **Windows Intune Agent Settings** and check the radio button next to the option for **Create and Deploy a Custom Policy**. Then click on the button titled **Create Policy** to proceed, as shown in the following screenshot:

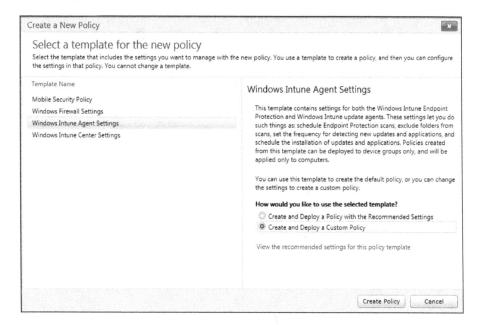

3. Your browser should now show you a policy template. Select **Endpoint Protection** from the center ribbon and locate the section titled **Endpoint Protection Service**. Click on the radio button next to the word **Yes** under the title **Enable Endpoint Protection**. This will force the removal of competing anti-malware products and the installation of Intune's Endpoint Protection client. The rest of the settings in this section should look familiar to you; they are the same set of options that you configure in SCEP when you are in the SCCM console. For now, just take the defaults and click on the **Save Policy** button to proceed, as shown in the following screenshot:

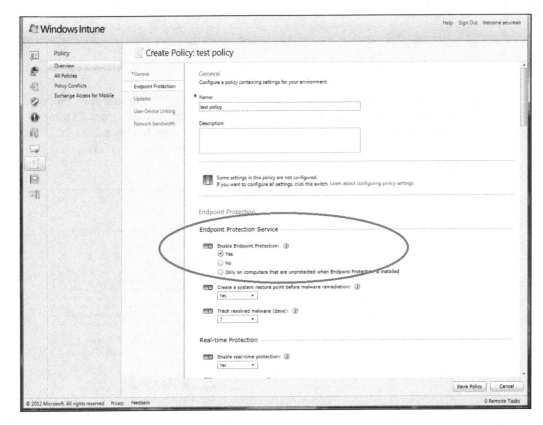

4. You will be prompted with the option to deploy the policy; select the **Yes** button to proceed, as shown in the following screenshot:

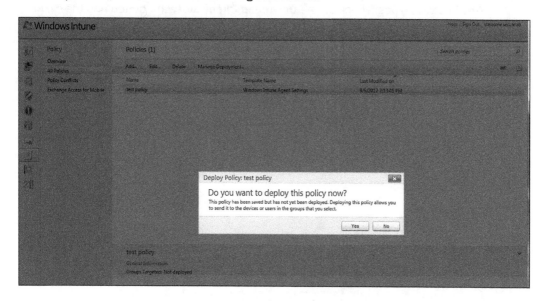

5. At this point, you can choose to deploy the policy to all of your Intune clients or a subset of clients. In this example, I will apply the policy to all clients. To do so, select **All Devices** from the column on the left-hand side and click on the **Add** button to move it over to the **selected groups** column. Then, click on **OK** to proceed, as shown in the following screenshot:

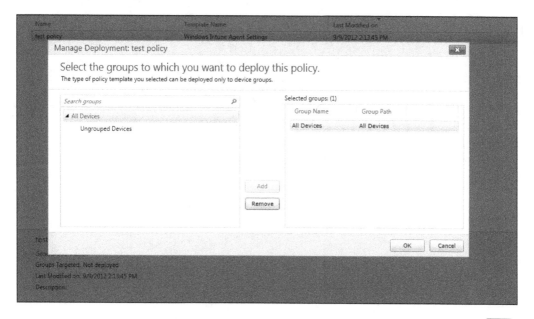

6. Next, we will install the Windows Intune client on your test PC. Click on the bottom button on left-hand side ribbon (the one with a screw driver and wrench) to get to the **Administration** page. Click on the **Download Client Software** button and the client software will download to your PC. Refer to the following screenshot:

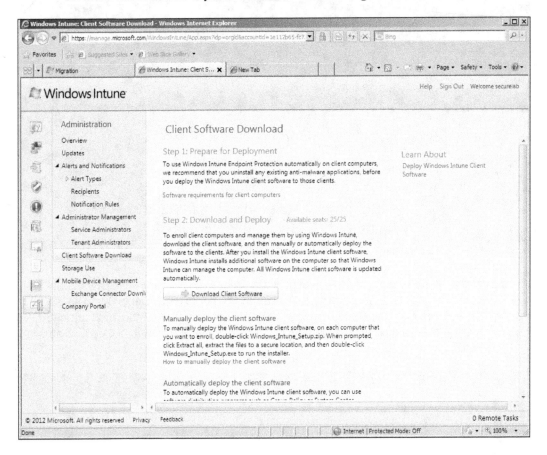

7. Once the download is complete, extract the zip file and run `Windows_Intune_Setup`, as shown in the following screenshot:

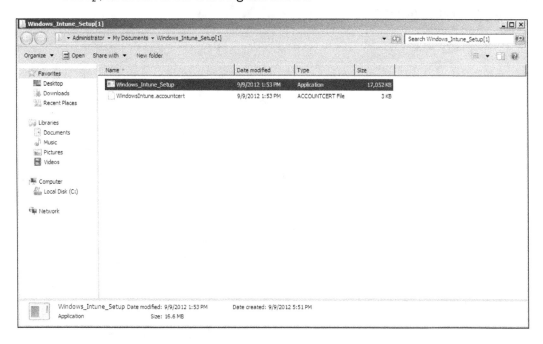

8. The **Windows Intune Setup** wizard should open. Click on **Next** on the first page to proceed, as shown in the following screenshot:

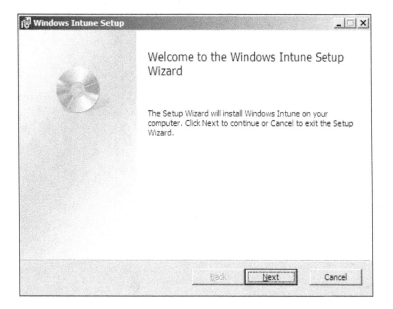

9. The installer will run for a few minutes; if all is successful, you will see a window stating the wizard has completed. Click on **Finish** to close it out, as shown in the following screenshot:

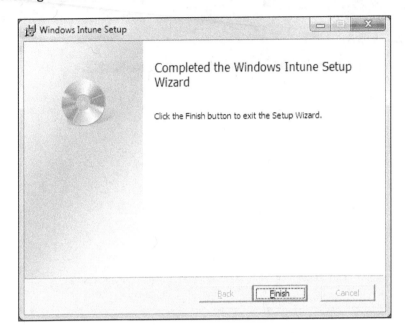

10. To verify whether the Intune client is on your PC, check the system tray. The Intune icon should now be there, as shown in the following screenshot:

11. After a few minutes, the **Windows Intune Endpoint Protection** client should also appear in the system tray. If you open it, you will notice that it is identical to the SCEP client except for the title on the top of the user interface. Refer to the following screenshot:

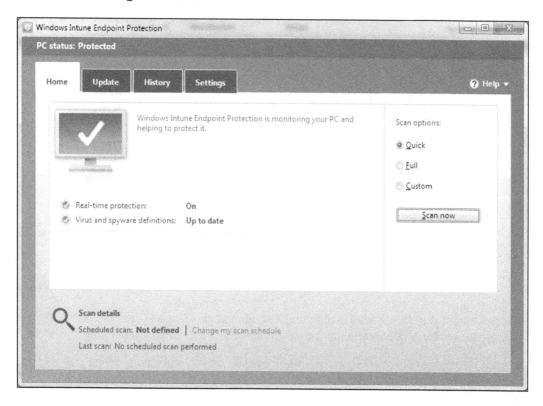

12. In order to test whether the Endpoint Protection client is working correctly and reporting to your Intune service in the cloud, I would suggest using the Eicar string to simulate a malware event. Eicar can be accessed at the following URL: http://www.eicar.org/

    This is a completely safe packet of data that is added to the definitions of most anti-malware products for testing purposes.

13. Once you have triggered the Eicar detection, log back into your Intune dashboard and click on the icon for **Endpoint Protection** (the blue and white shield) from the ribbon on the left-hand side. If your client reported correctly, you should see an `Eicar_test_file` detection, as shown in the following screenshot:

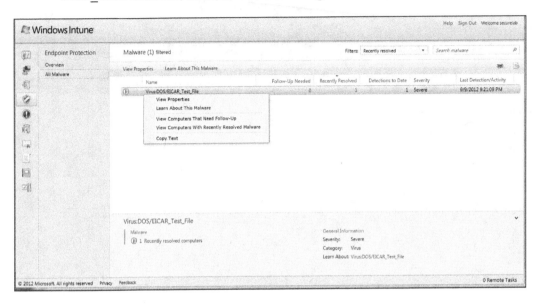

Windows Intune is a cloud-based management solution that offers a host of features, including the ability to deploy and manage a version of Microsoft's Endpoint Protection client.

Once the Intune client is on a PC, we can then deploy Endpoint Protection to the PC by setting a policy which requires the client to be already installed. After the client is installed, visibility into the state of the Endpoint Protection client as well as alerting for malware events, is accessible through the Intune management console.

In addition to being a great option for small to medium-sized organizations, some large companies may find Intune a suitable option for covering niche users. For example, if a large organization was to acquire a smaller organization and needed a stopgap solution to manage their systems, before their domains can be integrated into your root forest. Or, if for some political reason, part of an organization needed to be permanently managed at arm's length.

Index

Thank you for buying
Microsoft System Center 2012 Endpoint
Protection Cookbook

About Packt Publishing

Packt, pronounced 'packed', published its first book "*Mastering phpMyAdmin for Effective MySQL Management*" in April 2004 and subsequently continued to specialize in publishing highly focused books on specific technologies and solutions.

Our books and publications share the experiences of your fellow IT professionals in adapting and customizing today's systems, applications, and frameworks. Our solution-based books give you the knowledge and power to customize the software and technologies you're using to get the job done. Packt books are more specific and less general than the IT books you have seen in the past. Our unique business model allows us to bring you more focused information, giving you more of what you need to know, and less of what you don't.

Packt is a modern, yet unique publishing company, which focuses on producing quality, cutting-edge books for communities of developers, administrators, and newbies alike. For more information, please visit our website: www.PacktPub.com.

About Packt Enterprise

In 2010, Packt launched two new brands, Packt Enterprise and Packt Open Source, in order to continue its focus on specialization. This book is part of the Packt Enterprise brand, home to books published on enterprise software – software created by major vendors, including (but not limited to) IBM, Microsoft and Oracle, often for use in other corporations. Its titles will offer information relevant to a range of users of this software, including administrators, developers, architects, and end users.

Writing for Packt

We welcome all inquiries from people who are interested in authoring. Book proposals should be sent to author@packtpub.com. If your book idea is still at an early stage and you would like to discuss it first before writing a formal book proposal, contact us; one of our commissioning editors will get in touch with you.

We're not just looking for published authors; if you have strong technical skills but no writing experience, our experienced editors can help you develop a writing career, or simply get some additional reward for your expertise.

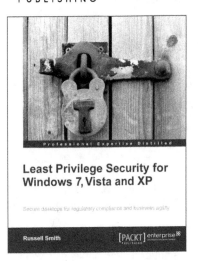

Least Privilege Security for Windows 7, Vista and XP

ISBN: 978-1-84968-004-2   Paperback: 464 pages

Secure desktops for regulatory compliance and business agility

1. Implement Least Privilege Security in Windows 7, Vista and XP to prevent unwanted system changes

2. Achieve a seamless user experience with the different components and compatibility features of Windows and Active Directory

3. Mitigate the problems and limitations many users may face when running legacy applications

Microsoft Data Protection Manager 2010

ISBN: 978-1-84968-202-2   Paperback: 360 pages

A practical step-by-step guide to planning deployment installation, configuration, and troubleshooting of Data Protection Manager 2010

1. A step-by-step guide to backing up your business data using Microsoft Data Protection Manager 2010 in this practical book and eBook

2. Discover how to back up and restore Microsoft applications that are critical in many of today's businesses

3. Understand the various components and features of Data Protection Manager 2010

4. Gain valuable insight into using Data Protection Manager through the author's real world experience

Please check **www.PacktPub.com** for information on our titles

Microsoft Forefront UAG 2010 Administrator's Handbook

ISBN: 978-1-84968-162-9   Paperback: 484 pages

Take full command of Microsoft Forefront Unified Access Gateway to secure your business applications and provide dynamic remote access with DirectAccess

1. Maximize your business results by fully understanding how to plan your UAG integration

2. Consistently be ahead of the game by taking control of your server with backup and advanced monitoring

3. An essential tutorial for new users and a great resource for veterans

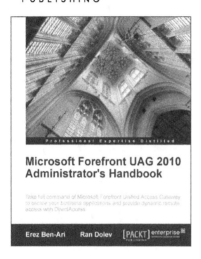

Microsoft Exchange 2010 PowerShell Cookbook

ISBN: 978-1-84968-246-6   Paperback: 480 pages

Manage and maintain your Microsoft Exchange 2010 environment with Windows PowerShell 2.0 and the Exchange Management Shell

1. Step-by-step instructions on how to write scripts for nearly every aspect of Exchange 2010 including the Client Access Server, Mailbox, and Transport server roles

2. Understand the core concepts of Windows PowerShell 2.0 that will allow you to write sophisticated scripts and one-liners used with the Exchange Management Shell

3. Learn how to write scripts and functions, schedule scripts to run automatically, and generate complex reports

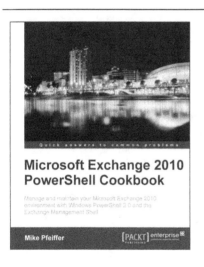

Please check **www.PacktPub.com** for information on our titles